Women in Control

Dilemmas of a Workers' Co-operative

JUDY WAJCMAN

The Open University Press
Milton Keynes

The Open University Press
A division of
pen University Educational Enterprises Limited
12 Cofferidge Close
Stony Stratford
Milton Keynes MK11 1BY, England

First Published 1983

British Library Cataloguing in Publication Data

Wajcman, Judy
  Women in control.
  1. Women in cooperative societies — Great Britain
  2. Fakenham Enterprises
  I. Title
  334'.6'0941   HD3175.A4

ISBN 0–335–10193–3

The publishers would like to thank the following:

Susan Shapiro for the photographs on p. 1 and p. 56; Pete Jefferies (I.F.L.) for the
photographs on p. 18 and p. 111; Times Newspapers Limited for the photograph
on p. 85; Eastern Counties Newspapers Limited for the photographs on p. 132 and
p. 156; Weidenfeld & Nicolson Limited for the diagram on p. 29 (taken from
Company Law and Capitalism, by Thomas B. Haddon, p. 396).

The cover photograph shows a group of women at Sexton's shoe factory in
Fakenham. (Taken from the TASS Journal, p. 23, August 1972.) The photograph
also appears on p. 37.

Text design by W.A.P.

Photoset by Enset Ltd,
Midsomer Norton, Bath, Avon

Printed by The Thetford Press Ltd, Thetford, Norfolk

Contents

Acknowledgements

The research on which this book is based originated as a Ph.D. thesis at Cambridge University. I was supported financially by the Fellows of St John's College, Cambridge, but also generously by my mother who would have preferred a grandchild for her money! Bob Blackburn supervised my thesis. He was unstinting in his interest and friendship then and has been since. Similarly, Tony Giddens and Colin Filer, each in their own way, cajoled and encouraged me to write, for which I am grateful. I would also like to thank Ken Prandy, Sandy Stewart and others in the Department of Applied Economics and in the Faculty of Economics in Cambridge for having provided such an enjoyable and stimulating workplace.

The adaptation of the thesis into a book was assisted by colleagues in the Sociology Department at Edinburgh University, but I would especially like to thank Donald MacKenzie. I am indebted to many friends and colleagues for helping me at various stages of the research and writing, in particular Jo Bradley, David Held, John Holmwood, Marthe Macintyre and Michelle Stanworth.

For a woman working in a predominantly male university and, for a period, in an exclusively male college, feminist support was indispensable. The Eden Street Women's Liberation Group and the Cambridge Women's Studies Group provided me with a sympathetic political and intellectual environment.

Books conventionally contain an acknowledgement to the author's 'wife'. I am pleased instead to acknowledge my friendships and a number of collective households in Cambridge, Edinburgh and London which have sustained, distracted and humoured me through the most trying times. Jenny Earle was an important part of the entire process of producing this book. She added a great deal to it and it would not have been possible without her.

Of course, my greatest debt is to the Fakenham women themselves; it is their story. I have not altered the names although, following their own usage, I have used only first names. The women would anyway be identifiable to those who know them. I hope they feel that I have told their story fairly and fully, and consider the time and companionship they gave to me worthwhile.

Abbreviations:

AUEW	Amalgamated Union of Engineering Workers
ASTMS	Association of Scientific, Technical and Managerial Staffs
ICOM	Industrial Common Ownership Movement
IWC	Institute for Workers' Control
NUFLAT	National Union of Footwear, Leather and Allied Trades
Sextons	Sexton, Son & Everard
Scott Bader	Scott Bader Commonwealth Ltd
TGWU	Transport and General Workers Union

Introduction

Women have conventionally been seen only in the home and heard not at all. Whether as cause or consequence, instances of working-class organisation on the part of men are undoubtedly better recorded than those of women. This fact sustains the belief that men set the pace in workplace militancy, in contrast with the deeprooted association between women and working-class quiescence. Even though the extensive participation of women in the workforce is now well documented, this popular conception of women as essentially family-oriented and men as essentially work-centred still holds sway. But women as well as men frequently engage in various forms of industrial action, although these are generally forgotten or obscured within days of their occurrence. What I have recorded in this book is an ordinary struggle of working-class women, extraordinary only in finding a place in our collective memory.

This is the story of a Norfolk shoe factory which became a co-operative through the collective action of the women who worked there. The co-operative, which became known as Fakenham Enterprises, was set up in 1972 when the workforce was threatened with redundancy. Before the occupation, Fakenham was a satellite factory of a Norwich shoe firm. It was closed down because it was not profitable. The initial response of the workers was to occupy the factory. There was a general upsurge of factory occupations in Britain at the time, but Fakenham was different; all the workers were women, and it was the first co-operative to grow out of these occupations. Having taken control of the factory, the women made substantial attempts to democratise their workplace. They instituted real changes in the internal organisation of the factory towards more collective decision-making, as well as sharing skills and work-tasks.

Women workers taking such innovative action in defence of their jobs gave the lie to the conventional wisdom that women are passive and home-centred. As a result the Fakenham women attracted a lot of attention in the women's movement. In response to a financial crisis in the factory which was publicised at the National Women's Liberation Conference in March 1975, members of the women's movement in Cambridge set up a Fakenham support group. Together with other members of this group I visited the factory several times in the following months, to see what we could do to help.

At the time my research interest was in the political consciousness of working-class women in employment. Fakenham Enterprises seemed an ideal setting for a case study. Here was a group of women in a work situation which could be expected to have a dramatic effect on their political consciousness.

Orthodox industrial sociology would find it hard to explain how working-class women in the heart of the Norfolk countryside succeeded in establishing a manu-facturing co-operative. If, as is generally assumed, working in a co-operative requires a higher level of commitment to work than a conventional job, this would be expected to entail a change in the women's domestic responsibilities. Otherwise, a women's co-operative would appear rather puzzling. In this book I try to explain the puzzle by exploring the interconnections between women's paid labour and sexual divisions within the family and tracing the significance of these factors for the political consciousness of working-class women.

The most appropriate method of data collection for a study such as I undertook is participant observation. It enables the researcher to obtain a full picture of what is being studied and to become thoroughly familiar with the surrounding environment—the town and the community. Furthermore, participant observation records people's practices, allowing one to observe the connection between what people say and what they actually do. It also enables the researcher to be sensitive to the meanings and values people express, and to try to understand their ambiguities, subtleties and contradictions. My use of direct quotations in this book attempts to convey some of these.

It was not difficult for me to become a participant observer at Fakenham. I went to live in Fakenham in June 1975, three years after the co-operative was set up, and worked there full-time for most of the period up to October. Hilary Knight, a sociology student and a feminist, agreed to spend a month there assisting me. Another feminist, Jackie Deere, was helping out in the factory when I arrived, though she planned to leave at the end of the month. According to Nancy, the worker–director of Fakenham Enterprises, she had been useful and Nancy was pleased at the prospect of a replacement. This seemed a perfect opportunity for us, and yet not so perfect. The first thing that struck both Hilary and myself during our initial visits was that we were always greeted by Nancy and Jackie, who would take us into the office to discuss the firm's problems. The possibility of replacing Jackie foreshadowed some of the difficulties I was to experience during my stay at Fakenham Enterprises. Jackie had spent most of her time at the factory in the office and was seen by the other women as Nancy's assistant. She often answered the telephone and had access to information simply by virtue of being in the office. I did not want to inherit her position because, in order to carry out my study, I wanted to work on the shopfloor with the women and talk to them. I wanted to avoid being identified with Nancy and restricted to the office. This was the classic problem of a researcher trying to avoid identification with the management, but in the strange context of a workers' co-operative.

After a few visits, I tentatively asked Nancy if I could work in the factory, explaining that I was doing research on women at work. I emphasised that I hoped she would ask the other women about it. She agreed to my working there, assured me that no-one would mind, and promised to ask the women anyway. I also spoke to a few of the women and they seemed pleased at the prospect of unpaid help. Our women's group had raised £80 for the factory and donated a calculator, so they knew we were acting in good faith.

As it turned out, I spent my first week at the factory without Hilary because she arrived late. I was nervous the day I arrived to start work—wondering what on earth I could do there. One skill I certainly did not have was operating a sewing-machine! I hung around the factory, did a few odd jobs and generally felt uncomfortable. The women were friendly and tried to put me at ease. I think they felt sorry for me. The role I quite consciously adopted, which was not hard in the circumstances, was that of a shy student. My enquiring attitude in this role was made even easier by my being Australian. The broad accent was a great help to me. It made my unfamiliarity with Norfolk life understandable, enabling me to ask all sorts of questions. My Australian identity also obscured my class background and oddities in my behaviour were generously accepted as a foreigner's idiosyncrasies. Lastly, I provided an endless stream of stories about life in Australia, offered in exchange for stories about their lives in Fakenham.

As it turned out, my inability to use a sewing-machine was also an advantage. The seventeen machinists working at the co-operative when I arrived spent most of the day at their machines. Doing odd jobs gave me the freedom I needed to move around the shopfloor. During my first few weeks at the factory about half the machinists were sewing pink and purple slipper uppers which were fluffy; the brightly coloured synthetic fluff got in the air and caused breathing irritation. Some of the women wore masks when machining, but they were hot and uncomfortable to wear—so most did not bother. The other machinists were sewing badges on to the sleeves of red parka-jackets. Speed, rather than intricate machining, was required for both these jobs. After they had sewn several items, the women would cut off the loose threads and pack the items in bundles. I often sat by a few machinists and did this job for them, folding the jackets into plastic bags, and stacking them near the fire exit, where work was collected and delivered.

The other five women, who could not machine, were known as bench-hands. Two of them sat at a bench knotting silver straps together—the uppers for evening shoes. This was a job that required nimble fingers and it took me longer to learn; I remained very slow at it. Two of the remaining women sat at the front bench doing a variety of non-machining jobs and the third, Nancy, often joined them when she was not in the office. Trying to make myself useful, I ran errands, did bits of shopping and sometimes made the tea, which was a great joke, as I myself drank lemon tea and always made a weak brew. More helpfully, I would collect some of the children from school if their mothers were having to work late to finish a contract on time.

I kept a comprehensive diary of events and conversations, which I diligently wrote up every evening. However, I also needed to collect more systematic information about the women and their husbands through interviews. Having worked full-time in the factory for about five months, I went back to Cambridge to draw up a semi-structured questionnaire. I had deliberately waited until towards the end of my stay to do these interviews, for two reasons. First, I felt confident that I would be able to construct appropriate questions arising out of my experience and knowledge of Fakenham. Second, I expected to have built up relationships with all the women. At first, through working with them, and then from meeting them around town and sharing their leisure activities, I did get to know the women on a personal basis and some of them invited me to their homes. This made interviewing easy and relaxed. While the factory was closed for its summer vacation, I returned to Fakenham and I visited all the women in their homes during the day. They were extremely helpful and many were glad of the opportunity to talk and be listened to. The interviews lasted several hours and covered many areas outside the scope of my specific questions.

This book primarily reflects the experience of women; but husbands were also interviewed, both because they were important to the women, and to elucidate aspects of working-class experience common to both sexes. In exploring the dynamics of family life it is essential to hear 'both sides of the story'. It is customary for the woman's version to be neglected, but in redressing this imbalance I did not want to leave out of account what the men had to say. I interviewed the husbands in the evening and, on the whole, they too were co-operative. The women had prepared the husbands for my visit, so we had good long talks and their wives usually left me alone with them. A few wives did stay during the interviews and, although this sometimes hindered my talking to their husbands, we often all got into interesting discussions. Only two of the husbands refused to talk to me.

The chapters that follow are organised in the following way. The first two chapters are intended to provide some background to the story that I am going to tell. In the opening chapter the position of women in employment, as well as their experience of paid work, is related to sexual divisions in the family. Chapter 2 discusses co-operatives within the framework of debates on common ownership, industrial democracy and workers' control.

An account of the events leading up to the establishment of a co-operative in Fakenham follows in the third chapter, where the narrative begins. The story is continued in Chapter 4, in which the first three years of the co-operative's existence are described, and which covers both the economic history of the enterprise and the development of its internal organisation. In Chapter 5 I describe the individual women taking part in the enterprise, and in Chapter 6, I return to the themes of Chapter 4, with an account based directly on my observations while working at Fakenham.

The focus shifts in Chapter 7 to the family and home lives of the workers. At this point in the book I start to draw out general conclusions from what happened in Fakenham. The final chapter explores the extent to which these women's experience of participation in a workers' co-operative affected their political consciousness.

1 Work and the Family

'The best of both worlds has come within their grasp,
if only they reach out for it'
                    (Myrdal and Klein, 1956: xvi).

'You can't have the best of both worlds'
                    (Fakenham worker).

The Optimistic View

In the post-war period, when the family and motherhood
were receiving a massive official boost, the increasing inte-
gration of *married* women into the workforce was seen as
both a dramatic and a potentially disruptive social change.
Early studies of women workers laid heavy emphasis on
how the families of these women were affected by their
employment. However, some writers at the time were

1

optimistic about the effect of these changes, arguing that
wives and mothers had a right to paid employment. For
example, Myrdal and Klein's book *Women's Two Roles,* first
published in 1956, took the view that women could successfully combine their roles as mothers and workers.

Many socialists and feminists have shared this optimism
about working mothers, arguing that having a paid job
outside the home is the key to women's liberation. Their
heritage is Engels' classic statement that: 'the first premise of
the emancipation of women is the re-introduction of the
entire female sex into public industry'. But this tradition has
more recently had to try to account for the extent to which
women's lives are dominated by the family.

Women's Two Roles provided the framework for a
number of sociological studies concerned with the position
of women in post-war Britain.[1] These have several
common features: they were all responses to what was
thought to be a recent and significant social development,
namely, the increasing proportion of married women
'going out to work'. Their 'social problem' perspective was
concerned with how adjustments might be made to accommodate this novel trend.[2] There was an implicit assumption, however, that generally life was 'getting better' with
industrialisation, which justified the further assumption
that, like everything else, women's position must also be
improving. The effects of industrialisation, such as smaller
families, better health, improved services and lighter
domestic chores, would enable wives and mothers to cope
with employment (Jephcott, Seear and Smith, 1962:135).
In fact, as Oakley has pointed out, the proportion of women
working, either as a percentage of the total labour force or as
a percentage of the total female population, hardly changed
between 1850 and 1950 (Oakley, 1981:145). In 1950 women
made up 30 per cent of the employed labour force, as they
did in 1850. Although most of the books I am discussing
provided a brief historical introduction, they displayed considerable ignorance of women's position before or during
'industrialisation', which makes it difficult to assess the
significance of the supposedly crucial changes they empha-

sised, such as the amount of domestic labour needed in the home, women's participation in production, and changes in sex roles and status.

These writers assume that 'work' is inherently pleasant, so that all a woman needs to forsake the home and enter the labour market is the opportunity to do so. Thus there is no longer:

> the need for women to make a fatal decision between irreconcilable alternatives. The Gordian knot of a seemingly insoluble feminine dilemma has been cut. The technical and social developments of the last few decades have given women the opportunity to integrate their two interests in Home and Work. . . . No longer need women forego the pleasures of one sphere in order to enjoy the satisfactions of the other
> *(Myrdal and Klein, 1956: xvi)*.

Such statements foster the suspicion that this literature confronts not the problems of women generally but, specifically, those of middle-class professional women who can enter the labour market for 'pleasure' and not out of financial necessity. This is not to say that working-class women do not feature in these studies, but rather that the discussion reflects a pre-occupation with middle-class values. These values are concerned with choice, equal opportunities, pursuit of a career, none of which are within the grasp of the majority of working-class or, indeed middle-class, women. There is nothing new about women going out to work. As we have seen, during this century women have always constituted at least 30 per cent of the labour force. For most women, the choice to work is still really no choice at all; many more families would be near the 'poverty line' without the wife's income.[3] Working-class women have long been accustomed to enjoying the 'satisfactions' of work. It is impossible to generalise about the reasons for women entering and leaving the labour market in a capitalist society without first understanding the class composition of this female labour force.

Overlooking such class distinctions, the 'two roles' literature embarks on a consideration of contemporary women's
greater motivation to go out to work. Although it is
assumed that any 'conflict' between women's two roles can
be resolved by technology and social reforms, most of the
writers would agree with Klein (1965 : 76) when she
concludes that:

> The outstanding impression gained from this survey is that
> women's lives, today as much as ever, are dominated by
> their role— actual or expected—as wives or mothers.

Thus women are seen as regarding their 'home' role as
primary and work as secondary and, when they do work, as
having a lower commitment to it than men. By concen-
trating on attitudes, these studies lose sight of the social
context which imposes limits on what women can do. To
understand the formation and significance of attitudes, we
need to examine the practical constraints which operate in
the domestic sphere; this will become clear in the case of the
Fakenham women.

To take the first point: whether and how far this 'natural'
tendency of women to put the 'home' first is a question of
need or pleasure is a moot point, and one not tackled by
these studies. Does the 'conflict' between women's two
roles just mean too much work, or does it mean that the two
kinds of work are, in themselves, incompatible? The
authors conceptualise this conflict in subjective terms, as an
individual 'feminine dilemma', ignoring its social basis.
Without a more precise understanding of the different kinds
of constraint on women in different social positions either to
'have to go out to work' or to say 'my family must come
first', we shall not know what such statements mean.

The second point, that of women's lower 'commitment'
to work, raises somewhat different problems. Certainly we
can get answers to the question: 'Do you think your family
is more important than your work?'—but when it comes to
elucidating the answers, in other words finding out what this
relative 'importance' consists of, we find that a host of

further questions are raised by this notion of 'commitment'. A woman may, for example, be 'committed' to housework either in the sense that she is house-proud, or in the sense that if she fails to do it, her husband will beat her. To make such a vaguely defined attitude a key variable in discussing the problems faced by working-class women in the factory and in the home is to obscure more important and more practical questions. What is to be done, for example, if your child comes out of school at 4 p.m. and there is no employment available that will enable you to be outside the school at that time? There will be a number of practical constraints on the choice of solutions to such a problem. Because women still bear primary responsibility for children, it is they who have to adjust their working lives to these obligations. Men do not have to make such adjustments; children's illness, for example, is not a legitimate or customary reason for men taking time off work. Does it follow that men are more committed to work? The notion of 'commitment' implies that the 'choices' made by married women—such as whether to work part-time or full-time—are a matter of will, rather than being largely *determined* by structured social arrangements.

The 'two roles' literature could be optimistic about married women's entry into the labour market because it ignored the gender-hierarchy that relegates women to the worst jobs. But an analysis of sexual divisions within the labour force paints a more pessimistic picture of how liberating paid employment for women can be. Feminists and others have welcomed the participation of women in industry, but their research has amply shown how women's paid work is likely to mirror the menial, unpaid work which they do in the home. This will emerge from what follows.

The Workforce: a few facts

The proportion of women in the British labour force increased from 32 per cent in 1951 to 40 per cent in 1980. This increase is mostly accounted for by an increase in the proportion of married women. In 1911 one in ten married women had a job; in 1951, one in four; in 1980, one in two. Today 60 per cent of married women work (HMSO, 1982).

The increase is due to demographic and economic changes. These include the reduction in age of marriage and in family size, as well as long-term shifts in the industrial structure away from manufacturing and towards services. Since the early sixties, there has been a massive reduction of jobs in the manufacturing industry, but this has been offset by the rise in service jobs. Three-quarters of all women workers are in the service industries, compared with just one-fifth in manufacturing. There are more women working in the education and health services alone than in the whole of manufacturing industry.

A second feature of female employment is the high proportion of women with part-time jobs. About 40 per cent of women workers work part-time, compared with only 5 per cent of employed men. More than 80 per cent of these part-time workers are married and the growth in part-time work is related to the increasing numbers of married women entering the labour force.

However, the increasing participation of women in paid work has had little impact on the segregated nature of their employment. In 1971, 61 per cent of all women workers were employed in ten census-classified occupations. In six of these (hand and machine sewers and embroiderers; typists and secretaries; canteen assistants and counter-hands; maids and related service workers; charwomen, office cleaners, etc; nurses) women comprised 90 per cent or more of the total numbers employed. Women are concentrated in low status occupations, where the work often involves the direct servicing of people's immediate needs. Thus 'the mass increase of women in paid labour has not involved the majority of women in forms of labour that clash with the cultural definitions of women's domestic identity' (Wainwright, 1978 : 171).

Nor has the increasing employment of women meant an improvement in their status. Quite the opposite. In 1966 72 per cent of all non-manual women workers were in

routine grades, compared with 51 per cent in 1921; 78 per
cent of manual women workers were in non-skilled jobs
compared with 64 per cent in 1921 (Westergaard and Resler,
1975). In short, occupational segregation in the labour
market means that few women are likely to be doing the
same work as men. For working-class women all jobs are
much the same, being essentially routine, low paid and
lacking advancement possibilities, so that the attractions of
work are mostly independent of the nature of the actual job.
Recognition of the limited job opportunities available
reduces women's involvement in work and reinforces
'commitment' to their domestic role.

Finally, in spite of increases in women's pay, they are still
paid significantly less than men. Although differentials in
average hourly earnings narrowed in the early seventies, the
gap is still large and has widened recently. The situation
facing part-time workers is particularly bad, as the association between low pay and part-time work is a very strong
one. In virtually every industry and occupation, part-time
work almost always means low-paid work, so badly paid in
fact as to be below the poverty level. The overall picture,
then, is one in which a significant proportion of the female
labour force receives extremely low wages.

The Labour Market

So when women enter paid work they do so under conditions quite different from those experienced by men.
There have been a number of attempts to explain these
sexual divisions in employment.[4] In socialist feminist literature a common theme concerns women's role in what Marx
described as the 'industrial reserve army'. This refers to the
groups of people who are sucked into employment in economic upswings and expelled again during recession; who
function, for example, to keep labour shortages from
sending wages skyhigh in booms. Women, it has been
argued, form just such a reserve army of labour, and substi-
tute for male labour when the latter is in short supply.

Empirical work has, however, shown that occupational specialisation by sex creates an inflexibility in the labour market so that women's and men's labour are not inter-changeable.

Other authors have argued that the labour market is better characterised by the existence of two non-competi-tive structured labour markets; that is, as a *dual labour market*. Jobs available in the primary sector are relatively secure, well paid, and tend to have good long-term pros-pects; those in the secondary sector are more precarious, low paid, and have poor working conditions. These con-ditions were certainly characteristic of the Fakenham women's working lives. By and large, women and men are simply not competing for the *same* jobs. The primary labour market is largely inhabited by men. According to this approach, women's disadvantaged position in the labour market is accounted for by their confinement to the second-ary sector.

However, this is a description of the present structure of the labour market rather than an explanation of how it emerged. The most obvious explanation is in terms of skill. Women, it is said, are unskilled—hence their confinement to the secondary labour market. It is certainly true that women's work tends to be classified as unskilled in official classifications. But the crucial question is how definitions of skill are established. To take a simple example, women who assemble digital watches and pocket calculators require con-siderable manual dexterity ('nimble fingers'), the capacity for sustained attention to detail and excellent hand–eye co-ordination. Yet these capacities are not defined as 'skills'.

How has it come about that women have failed to achieve recognition of the skills required by their work? The basis for distinctions of skill in women's and men's work is not a simple technical matter. It is a question of workers' collective efforts to protect and secure their conditions of employment—by defining their jobs as skilled and defend-ing that skill to the exclusion of outsiders. This process has shaped much of what makes up the 'primary' sector of the labour market. These efforts have been made predominantly by and on behalf of the male working class. They have been directed against employers who have regularly tried to find ways of substituting cheaper workers for expensive skilled labour. But men's resistance has also operated against women's interests. Defending skill, preventing 'dilution', has almost always meant blocking women's access to an occupation (Phillips and Taylor, 1980; Cockburn, 1983).

This discussion of the nature of skill shows that women's relation to production cannot be explained simply by the workings of labour markets. Why should it be *women* who necessarily occupy a particular place within the reserve army or the secondary labour market? I shall argue that the answer lies in the power of men over women. This 'patri-archal' power finds expression in public organisations and the workplace, but has its roots in the home. So we turn now to the organisation of domestic labour, the ideology of domesticity and its consequences for women's position in production.

Housework

According to popular belief, the result of the increasing proportion of married women in paid employment is that marriage is becoming an egalitarian relationship. For example, *The Symmetrical Family* by Young and Willmott has perpetuated the optimism of the earlier 'two roles' literature about women's changing role resulting from their entry into the workforce. This increased marital symmetry, in the sense of a changed division of labour in the home, means that husbands do a lot more housework: 'even clothes–washing and bed-making, still ordinarily thought of as women's jobs, were frequently mentioned by hus-bands as things they did as well' (Young and Willmott, 1975 : 94). However, these authors still maintain that most married women are less committed to their jobs: work means something different for women and does not reflect a weaker commitment to their domestic role. For Young and

Willmott, a greater sharing of domestic labour between husbands and wives follows necessarily from the fact that more married women work outside the home.

But do women abandon housework when they enter the labour force? Or is there any truth in a related claim, that the introduction of labour-saving devices in the home has reduced the time spent on housework? In fact, there is little evidence supporting either claim.[5] The sexual division of labour within the family is not transformed by women going out to work. Rather, women's 'lesser commitment' to their jobs may simply reflect their acquisition of a paid work role *in addition* to their domestic one. Oakley (1974) argues that while *attitudes* towards the sharing and organisation of housework have become more egalitarian, changes in *behaviour* have been much less marked. Husbands do not share domestic tasks equally with their wives. Rather, women remain *responsible* for housework and childcare, and husbands 'help' wives to do their domestic work.

The 'domestic labour debate' which occupied many writers between 1972 and 1978 decisively established the crucial importance of this work by women for the survival of capitalist society. Were it not for women's unpaid labour in the home, wages would have to be much higher as men would have to pay on the market for the services they needed. Otherwise, men's standard of living would be much lower. A popular poster captured the message. It showed a line of (male) workers filing into a factory, working for their employer, coming out at the other end and being fed, clothed and comforted by women. 'Capitalism depends on domestic labour too' read the caption. 'Housework' was not trivial—it was domestic labour, on a par with wage labour in its importance.

But, although the analogy between domestic work and paid work is important, ultimately it becomes misleading.[6] The crucial point is that capitalism has *separated* the two. The 'family' is separate from 'industry', the 'private' from the 'public', 'reproduction' from 'production'—separations which made no sense in a pre-industrial household economy. The conditions under which the two forms of labour (domestic and waged) are now performed are quite different. It is on the basis of marriage and motherhood, not of the wage, that the housewife's work is related to social labour. And neither marriage nor motherhood are, by any stretch of the imagination, simply 'economic' relations. An understanding of them, and of the social relations of domestic production, cannot be achieved simply by applying the analogy of the relation between worker and employer.

However, economic relations are still important. Even when married women are employed there is still a financial basis for marriage as a relationship of inequality. As we have seen, there is an especially exploitative relationship between employers and their women employees—in particular mothers, who generally work part-time or as home-workers. Most married women workers barely earn a subsistence wage and the Fakenham women were no exception. This leaves them dependent on their husbands' wages for part of their living costs and those of their children. The impossibility of economic independence, even for employed women, perpetuates the domestic division of labour in its present form.

The Ideology of the Family

Discussions about the nature of housework do not explain the origins and persistence of the understanding that this work is *women's* work. We need such an explanation to account for the different involvement of women and men in paid labour. Although working-class women and men have low expectations of work, this does not mean the same for men as for women. Some married women are able to choose whether they take a job or not—no such choice is normally open to men. The expectation that men have to have a regular job and that women have to see that the children are cared for is reflected in social arrangements and becomes the basis of constraints. Furthermore, married men see themselves and are seen as the 'breadwinners', and supporting their families is largely what gives work meaning for them. Men's social identity within the family is shaped by this ideology of the 'male breadwinner'. For women, the work role as a source of social identity is largely replaced by the domestic roles of wife and mother.

To appreciate the primacy women themselves give to the domestic sphere, we turn briefly to Oakley's character-isation of the feminine role.[7] In *Housewife,* she examines the emergence and nature of the 'modern housewife' role, and the exclusive allocation of housework and childcare to women. The essential constituents of femininity identified by Oakley are 'domesticity' and 'maternity'; the sense of 'being a housewife' is deeply rooted in feminine self-identity. 'It is the interaction of the two which distinguishes the situation of the female (housewife–wife–mother) from that of the male (husband–father)' (Oakley, 1976 : 78). Essentially, Oakley sees marriage as a relationship of in-equality, in which the domestic oppression of women as unpaid labourers, housewives and childrearers is main-tained and reproduced. She sees the relations of dominance and dependence structured by the institution of marriage as stemming from the sexual division of labour within the family. This concept of the housewife role as an amalgam of domesticity and maternity may help us to understand why women with a 'work role' should continue to be dominated by their 'home role'. Women in the labour force may be 'psychologically involved' with the housewife role in such a way that all experience, including that in the workplace, is filtered through a primarily domestic perspective.

Psychological identification with the domestic world is, then, one determinant of women's 'commitment' to housework, as well as their 'motives' for entering paid employment. However, we must beware of accepting explanations of, for example, women's low job expec-tations couched solely in psychological terms. These expectations must themselves take account of women's economic position in the family and in the labour market. In particular, married women's experience of severely limited job opportunities shape their orientations to wage labour, irrespective of their attachment to the domestic–maternal role. It is the grounding of women's expectations of work in their actual experience, both in paid employment and in the family, that this discussion has tried to emphasise.

Life Cycle

Of course, this experience of employment and of the family is not the same for all women. In particular, it is very different for women of different ages. Life cycle changes are crucial to the way in which domestic circumstances affect work experience, attitudes and behaviour. We can distinguish five typical stages in the life cycle in relation to work-life (Beynon and Blackburn, 1972 : 24). First, there is the time before marriage, when a woman's financial responsibilities are small; then there are the years of marriage before having children, followed by the period when the children are young and the mother is at home to care for them; as the children grow older, and make greater demands on the parental income, she may return to work; finally, the children grow up and become independent, the mother is free to work if she wishes, the financial pressures are eased and the next landmark is retirement. The life cycle takes a cultural rather than a 'natural' form; there are social expectations of appropriate behaviour at each stage. We need to examine carefully the developmental element of family life and its consequences for women's relation to employment.

Obvious though this point seems, it tends to be neglected when sociologists discuss women workers. When examining their own data, Beynon and Blackburn really distinguish only between two groups: single women and married women with children. The same can be said of the studies of factory workers by Lupton (1963), Cunnison (1966), and more recently by Pollert (1981) and Porter (1982).[8]

These books all contain similar observations about the distinctive expectations which the two groups of women

have of employment. To quote from Beynon and Blackburn's discussion of a group of women, the majority of
whom were single and aged under 30:

> Most of the women who worked full-time did have to
> support themselves, however, so good pay and security
> were quite important to them. . . . their interest in security
> lay between that of the part-time women and that of the
> men . . . Their main attachment to their jobs lay in friend-
> ships with workmates (149).

They contrast this group with those who worked part-time,
all of whom were married with children:

> They worked to supplement the family income but within
> the range open to them the actual amount was not so
> important. The other main reason for working was escape
> from the loneliness at home to the companionship of work
> (147).

The authors conclude that neither group had high expectations about the intrinsic nature of their jobs, but that the
expectations of the full-time group were higher than those
of the part-timers. For the married women, working hours
that could be conveniently fitted in with their family
commitments were their main concern: 'beyond this their
expectations were very low'.

When I go on to consider the Fakenham workers, further
significant distinctions *within* the category of married
women will be drawn. In order to explore the differences in
orientations of women employees beyond those depending
on whether they are single or married with children, it is
necessary to treat the household economy seriously, by
examining the distribution of labour and resources within it
overtime. Otherwise, it is unclear what the life cycle means
for women, apart from a general reference to responsibility
for childcare. We need to take account of the psychological
and ideological aspects, as well as the economic or
'material'. The life cycle involves changes in how women

see themselves, as well as changes in their financial circumstances. And all these things are important for women's
relationship to and experience of employment.

It would be wrong, however, to give the impression that
life cycle changes impinge only on women's work; they are
also of fundamental importance in *men's* relationship to their
work. For both women and men, the experience of work is
mediated by their place in the family. But women and men
have very different experiences of the family. The way
reproduction and childcare are currently organised means
that the life cycle affects men largely in terms of financial
strain, rather than imposing the necessity of part-time work
to allow for childcare. This is reflected in the fact that
'working fathers' or 'married men going out to work' have
not been the subject of much anxious enquiry. And while
the dramatic increase in unemployment has provoked
comment on the importance of paid work for women, the
impact of unemployment on men's orientation to the
family has gone largely unremarked.

Women and Men

Over the last decade or so feminists, in focussing on
women's subordination, have necessarily stressed what is
specific about the position of women in paid work. But this
healthy emphasis on the difference between the actual
situations of women and men has resulted in an unfortunate
tendency to treat each sex as a homogeneous group. The
analysis of work has proceeded along sex-differentiated
lines, so that certain factors have become defined as
appropriate in the study of either women's work or men's
work, but not in both.[9] Typically, a 'gender model' has
been adopted for the study of women's work. In this model,
women's relation to employment is treated as derived from
their family experiences. Simultaneously, men's work is
analysed using a 'job model', in which men's work attitudes
and behaviour are seen solely as the consequence of their
occupational experiences.

This approach prevents us from understanding *either* women's work *or* men's work. Neither the family nor gender *fully* accounts for women's experience of work. If the gender model is the only analytic tool we apply, we are often left asking the spurious question 'what makes women workers different from workers in general?', with the latter group assumed implicitly to be male. For men's relation to work cannot be understood in isolation from their family responsibilities and privileged domestic position. Rather than a gender model for women's work, and a job model for men's work, we need a gender *and* job model applied to both men's *and* women's work.

A recurring theme in discussions of women's employment is their commitment to work or lack of it. These discussions have suffered from the exclusive application of a gender model to women's work. It is still being said of women workers that 'family and homes were the important things in their lives . . . you want a happy home life to make up for the work'.[10] While the family still is in certain respects the area of prime importance for women, such statements are unlikely in fact to distinguish women from men. In a recent survey of unqualified male manual workers in a variety of jobs, almost 90 per cent of married respondents rated a 'good family life at home' above enjoyment of their work life.[11] That men may also put 'home' first is completely ignored. This is so even though it is now widely acknowledged that a serious limitation of existing studies of male manual workers is their failure to go 'beyond the factory gates', relying instead on information collected at the workplace.

If an account incorporating both gender and job factors was presented of men's work, the fact that women and men have different experiences of the family would emerge more clearly. This might also highlight important similarities between groups of male and female workers. For example it *may* be that, in terms of their experience of paid work, full-time women workers without dependent children have more in common with similarly placed full-time men than with part-time women workers. Such possibilities are ignored if we consider women in the light of their family identity and men in that of their work identity.

The problem has a parallel in discussions of class consciousness. Hand in hand with the assertion that women give priority to the home goes the assumption that women's class consciousness lags behind that of the male working class. The latter is implicitly taken as the 'standard' from which deviations are measured, but its character is never explored. This is true even of authors who are concerned to demolish the myth of women's conservatism — the male paradigm is seldom acknowledged, let alone demolished.

We are told in one study, for example, that even women whose husbands were shop stewards mostly rejected unions as irrelevant to them and as more to do with men. Significantly, this is taken as a sign of their backwardness rather than their astuteness (Porter, 1982). The difference between women's 'regressive' attitudes and the men's 'radical' ones is accounted for by reference to the women's family position. Women's consciousness is different from men's and it is argued that this can be explained by gender. But the differences between women's and men's experiences at the workplace may be just as important as gendered family roles in accounting for differences in their consciousness.[12] Rather than contrasting women's deficient consciousness with an undefined male working-class consciousness, it would be more illuminating to compare working-class women's consciousness with that of men occupying similarly low-paid non-union sector jobs. By assuming that it is legitimate to compare the consciousness of all women and all men, we ensure that gender *per se* emerges as the crucial determinant of women's consciousness. And so the myth of women's inherent conservatism endures.

2 Co-operatives: an experiment in workers' control

British Producer Co-operatives

There is nothing new about co-operatives. Several hundred were set up in Britain during the nineteenth century, although few of them survive today. The ideals of the British co-operative movement are traceable to the early 19th-century proposals of Robert Owen and others for factory communities, and later to the more limited plans of the Christian Socialists for the establishment of producer co-operatives. However, retail consumer co-operatives, and agricultural marketing and service co-operatives, have been the only forms to establish themselves on a widespread and lasting basis. The retail consumer co-operatives developed out of the friendly and provident societies formed in many working-class communities from the middle of the 18th century onwards to provide protection for members against sickness and unemployment in the new industrial conditions. In establishing the first enduring retail co-operative in 1844, the Rochdale Pioneers extended the already established principles of co-operation from communal thrift and mutual assurance to the supply of everyday necessities at fair prices from a society shop. The Pioneers also established a co-operative cotton factory in 1854. Initially, the 100 or so workers in co-operative constituted the majority of its shareholders. As a result of a boom in the cotton market in 1859, the factory was successful and began to attract conventional investors, who were not involved in the co-operative movement and did not work in the mill. By the end of 1860, the co-operative had 1,400 shareholders, of whom only 200 worked in it. Thus, within a year, the co-operative was transformed into a joint stock company. From the 1860s onwards, a number of producer co-operatives sprang up, sometimes as a result of a strike, often due to the assistance of a wealthy individual or a trade union. Many soon degenerated into little more than participative capitalist firms, however, and there was little communication between them.

Between 1882 and 1893 there was an enormous expansion, and the number of producer co-operatives increased more than sixfold. In 1881 there were 13 co-operatives; by 1893, there were 113 (Jones, 1976 : 36). This expansion was concentrated in three industries: clothing, printing and boots and shoes. There were also a number of ventures into co-operative building and construction, with some short-lived successes. But clothing, printing and boots and shoes always seem to have accounted for at least 60 per cent of the enterprises in existence at any one time. Concentration in a narrow range of industries, and modest commercial success, characterised this phase in the history of producer co-operatives. Throughout the 1880s and 1890s the initiative for these came, without exception, from working-class people or institutions, relying on the co-operative consumer movement for markets. Although there were numerous attempts to go beyond the original scope of handicraft enterprises, including ventures into textiles, mining and even shipbuilding, the shortage of capital and technically competent management prevented the establishment of permanent co-operatives in industry generally. Further, the producer organisations which were viable tended to degenerate into some form of joint stock enterprise. None of these co-operatives attempted to ensure that ownership and control were vested only in the workforce. Characteristically, they were a combination of internal and external ownership and control. Rather than being model co-operatives, they included in their work-forces workers with no shares and thus no membership.

In the twentieth century co-operative enterprises of this kind have been largely on the defensive, and by the end of 1975 there were only 17 remaining. While the oldest of these was established in 1874, none has been set up since 1950. They are mainly in the East Midlands, still concentrated in the clothing, footwear and printing trades, and are nearly all small businesses—in 1975 only one had more than 200 employees, and only six had a turnover of more than £½ million. Where technological change is relatively slow, making high capital investment for re-equipment unnecessary, small labour-intensive units can be fairly efficient, which perhaps explains their survival.

It has indeed been argued that some of the earlier producer co-operatives lasted longer, on average, than small private companies (Jones, 1976). This still begs the question of how to measure their success. In discussing the success of a co-operative, as distinct from a conventional business, the extent of worker participation in ownership and control must be a paramount consideration. The evidence suggests that few of these co-operatives were completely self-governing and that the extent of worker participation varied greatly. More commonly profitability is taken as a measure of success. But if these co-operatives were relatively successful as small firms, how is this explained? It is widely acknowledged today that co-operatives endure because bad years are absorbed by worker–shareholder sacrifices. For this to be possible they must work with a different idea of economic viability. Unless it is clear what criteria are being used, any assessment of the early period is bound to be inconclusive. The common view that the history of British producer co-operatives has been one of unmitigated failure is perhaps too gloomy. However, whether it is judged in terms of economic survival or workers' participation, it is no success story.

The situation today reflects the same basic problems. Contemporary producer co-operatives fall broadly into two categories. Those associated with the common ownership movement have grown out of a tradition of paternalistic business management, imbued with Quaker ideals. The others, set up in response to redundancies, have been characterised as 'the new worker co-operatives'. Fakenham Enterprises, fitting into neither category, has features of both: set up as a result of factory closure, it was nevertheless a member of the Industrial Common Ownership Movement. Before turning to worker co-operatives, I shall provide a brief account of that movement.

Common Ownership

The common ownership movement developed in the 1960s and 1970s, although the pioneer firm in this field was formed in 1951, when Ernest Bader, a Quaker and Christian Socialist, transferred ownership of his successful chemical firm to its workforce. A few years later, in 1958, he founded the Industrial Common Ownership Movement (ICOM)— whose objective was to launch new enterprises and transform existing ones into common ownership. A few other privately owned firms followed Bader's lead and by the end of 1976, ICOM had ten member companies, employing some 1200 people, with a combined turnover of about £20 million (Oakeshott, 1978 : 74). The Scott Bader Commonwealth Ltd. (hereafter referred to as Scott Bader) is by far the largest firm, accounting for £15 million of this turnover figure. Most of the other ICOM companies are small, with fewer than 50 employees.[1] A significant difference between ICOM companies and the earlier producer co-operatives is that their membership is open only to the workers in the enterprise, although there are several alternative structures. The most common structure is a two-tiered one, in which all shares in the company are owned by a holding company, limited by guarantee, and democratically controlled by a membership restricted to people who work for the operating company.

Scott Bader, the best known and most commercially successful member of ICOM, had a major influence on developments at the Fakenham factory. Its founder believed that the principle of common ownership in industry represented 'essential steps towards a true Christian industrial and social order'. The Scott Bader constitution embodied this philosophy, as the following excerpt illustrates:

> Our purpose in making our stand is for a better, peaceful, industrial and social order, for which purpose we believe that we must obey the simple laws of Christianity in our daily lives and present an alternative to a war-based capitalist economy on the one hand, and to communism on the other.

Scott Bader, although a co-operative venture, is organised along fairly traditional lines with a pyramidal management structure, balanced and checked by a series of elected workers' committees. Nominal control is exercised by employees as members of the holding company through elected representatives on the Board of Directors. Wage differentials have been reduced, but there is still a maximum ratio of 7:1 between the highest and the lowest pay. The constitution ensures that a proportion of each year's profits must be reinvested in the firm, while the rest are distributed as bonus payments to the workers and to charity.

The Quaker connections of this founding company lend the common ownership movement an appearance of latter-day Owenism. Their 1972 pamphlet begins:

> We believe that the increasing tensions of our industrial society can only be resolved by changing the whole basis of industrial ownership so as to establish community of interest in place of conflict.

In the hope of demonstrating the viability of workers' control within a market economy, new common ownership enterprises are financed with profits from member firms.

Ownership by the workers of the means of production might be expected to change fundamentally the social relations of the enterprise; especially the roles of management and unions and the relations of workers to each other. However, a survey of ICOM companies reveals that their practices fall well short of their common-ownership ideals. For instance, under the present constitution at Scott Bader, the son of the founder is Company Chairman for life and retains considerable power. The trade union movement has not been involved in the establishment of ICOM, and although union officials are active on an individual basis, unionisation in its member companies is relatively low. Not only do trade unions play little part in determining pay and conditions in these enterprises, but the extent of workers' control is severely limited. Ultimate control is not exercised by the representative bodies. And it is control rather than formal collective ownership that counts in the actual organisation of an enterprise.[2] Originating mainly in initiatives from above, these co-operatives operate a system that can best be described as benevolent paternalism: more an extensive participation in management than worker self-management. They have consequently failed to generate much enthusiasm at the shop-floor level.

Worker Co-operatives

The traditional co-operative movement has played almost no part in the development of the new worker co-operatives. The early 1970s in Britain witnessed a series of factory occupations, triggered off by the 1971 work-in at Upper Clyde Shipbuilders. The impulse behind this movement was the defence of the 'right to work'. Unlike their leaders, rank and file trade unionists became increasingly unwilling to negotiate redundancy agreements as they realised that alternative employment was not available. Workers were forced to seek more effective means of fighting redundancy than the traditional strike. As part of this search for a new strategy, there were various attempts to create worker co-operatives, reviving failed businesses under the self-management of their employees. Yet, unlike the earlier producer co-operatives, none of these seem to have been the product of strong initial feelings in favour of the co-operative form. Most of the workers concerned apparently were not asserting their right to self-management. Rather, they were willing to consider any proposals which ensured their employment. Had it been possible to persuade former owners to reverse close-down decisions, or to persuade new capitalists to move in, the workers would have accepted such solutions. Although it was not an end in itself, increasing their control became for the workers involved a condition of securing their employment. The first such occupation to result in the formation of a producer co-operative was at Fakenham.

Other worker co-operatives, although formed later, have been more widely discussed. Until the advent of the 1974 Labour Government, these remained small-scale initiatives. With bankruptcies rapidly becoming a feature of British manufacturing industry, the Secretary of State for Industry, Wedgwood Benn, inherited a variety of problems of factory closure. When he took office, there was a major dispute in the motorcycle industry, where the Norton Villiers Triumph factory at Meriden was under occupation. In July of that year, the former Fisher Bendix factory at

Merseyside, which had already been the scene of a pro-
longed sit-in in 1972, was once again occupied. Earlier, in
March, the *Scottish Daily Express* in Glasgow had been
closed and the workers had organised a sit-in. As a result of
lobbying, the government was persuaded to finance
workers' co-operatives in each of these three enterprises. It
agreed to lend £3.9 million to the former Fisher Bendix
factory, which started up again as the Kirkby Manufacturing and Engineering Company. Of this loan, £1.8 million
was paid to the Receiver in order to clear the liabilities of the
old company. In addition, the government agreed to put up
almost £5 million for the Meriden motorcycle factory, and
to offer £1.75 million to the workers' co-operative at what
was to become the *Scottish Daily News,* on condition that
they raised the balance of the necessary capital. At the time
of writing, in 1982, only Meriden is still operating. The
Kirkby co-operative finally closed down early in 1979,
while the *Scottish Daily News* lasted only six months.[3]

The idea of forming a co-operative at Kirkby emerged
from talks between the Secretary of State for Industry and
the union convenors, Jack Spriggs (AUEW) and Dick
Jenkins (TGWU). As indicated earlier, the workers
accepted it not because of a political commitment, but as an
expedient means of keeping the business open. When the
co-operative was set up, as well as representing the workers
on the shop stewards' committee, Spriggs and Jenkins
became the sole directors and ultimate controllers of the
company. Although this was done to prevent conventional
managerial directors reasserting control, the merging of
union officials into management inhibited the workers
from making the traditional union response to unresolved
grievances. It seems that Spriggs and Jenkins basically ran
the co-operative while the Works Council assumed a purely
nominal role, with little initiative coming from the shop-
floor workers. Worker commitment to co-operative
practices was generally lower than at Meriden—one
indication of this was the maintenance of a fairly conventional wage structure.

As the longest lasting and most democratic of these three

co-operatives, the Meriden venture is worth looking at in some detail. It was set up in March 1975 with a workforce of 162, which quickly expanded to one of over 700. Briefly, the story began in September 1973, when the management of the Triumph motorcycle works abruptly announced that the factory at Meriden would be closed and all 1,750 workers made redundant. The workforce, led by TGWU convenor Denis Johnson, immediately imposed an embargo on the removal of motorcycles and parts from the works—assets worth several million pounds. They staged a work-in, followed by a sit-in which lasted 18 months, until the co-operative was established. The idea of setting up a co-operative, conceived by the TGWU divisional organiser, received an immediate and enthusiastic response from the workforce. It was launched with a government grant and loan. The first directors were the eight shop stewards' convenors. Two outside part-time advisers were also appointed. Directors and workers alike were paid at the same rate, then £50 a week—a figure well below the local average wage. More workers joined the co-operative later, despite the substantial drop in wages this entailed. A single rate, eliminating the traditional differentials between skilled and unskilled, was a feature of the co-operative's wages policy from the start.

The reform of working practices involved the replacement of supervisors and foremen by 'organisers' and co-ordinators, who were appointed by the shop steward–directors and appear to have exercised a less supervisory role. It also meant the end of job delimitation based on previous collective bargaining practices, and much greater flexibility in movement from job to job. Productivity increased sharply, it is generally claimed, by about 50 per cent. The reforms in working practices were undertaken largely in relation to existing equipment. Changes requiring large expenditure have never been financially possible and this has been a limiting factor.

The Meriden co-operative inherited a dedicated workforce. Proud of their product and confident in their craftsmanship, many of them had worked at the factory for many years:

> Families have served apprenticeships at 'The Triumph', man and boy. Those who have hung on (while trying to establish the co-operative) have worked there for 10, 20 and even 40 years. They 'live, breathe and dream motorcycles'
> *(Huckfield, 1974 : 29)*.

Perhaps this long service and an identification with the product contributed to the egalitarian structure of pay and supervision.

Despite the low wages paid, the co-operative has never been profitable—it recorded a deficit of £1.2 million in its first year, and one of £1.3 million in 1977–78 (Taylor, 1979). To survive, it had to accept major redundancies of about 200 in 1979 and a further 300 in 1980. It has been hit hard by the effect of the rise in sterling against the dollar on imports to the North American market. It ran into severe difficulties in 1977, and hired a professional management team, paid at competitive rates. The members have since reintroduced skill differentials and an incentive scheme to improve output and encourage craftsmen not to leave. A grading system has also been introduced, although the differentials are still much lower than in private industry, with the top grades getting appreciably less than average rates, and the bottom more. These developments have eroded the egalitarian pay approach of the early days. Thus the co-operative has had to make fundamental compromises, which have reduced workers' control to little more than a formality.

Although the ICOM companies and the worker co-operatives together largely make up the contemporary producer co-operative movement, they have less in common than this might suggest. Many ICOM companies were successful businesses before becoming co-operatives, while the worker co-operatives grew out of factory closures. In such cases, co-operative ownership could not reverse the decline of firms which capitalists had failed to run at a profit. Heavily undercapitalised and in a bad market position, they were handicapped from the start. In these unfavourable economic conditions, managerial expertise was especially crucial. But, whereas the management structure of Scott Bader, for example, was largely that of its originating private company, the worker co-operatives were deprived of the management skills needed by any business enterprise. On the other hand, as a result of the shop-floor trade unionism vital to their establishment, these co-operatives did, at least initially, involve a greater degree of worker self-management. Sustaining such practices has, however, proved extremely difficult for co-operatives operating in a competitive capitalist market. Typically, the co-operative may be forced to choose between operating at a loss and reducing wages, its survival thus premised on self-exploitation, or accepting redundancies—which it was set up to avert. In its efforts to defend jobs, the workforce may find itself accepting wages and conditions which would not be tolerated in a private company. In contrast, the ICOM companies, which have been commercially successful, hardly represent an 'alternative' method of organising industry.

The Politics of Co-operatives

The emergence of the new worker co-operatives in the 1970s elicited responses from almost the whole British political spectrum—from the revolutionary left to the Conservative Party.[4] This was the political context for the Fakenham co-operative. Then, as now, support for co-operatives was not divided along party political lines; but people of different political persuasions do embrace differing conceptions of co-operatives. To some, co-operatives are a model of popular private enterprise, while to others they represent an alternative to private enterprise, a step towards a new society. Such a divergence of views must be due partly to the lack of a sufficiently specific definition of a co-operative.

For purposes of clarification, the legal definition of a

co-operative may prove a useful starting point. In terms of their legal status, co-operatives are enterprises where membership and participation in profit are linked to the provision of labour or produce or the use of facilities, rather than the contribution of capital. The essence of this approach, as shown in the diagram below, is to deny capital the right to anything but a 'reasonable' return at a fixed rate of interest. Any profit remaining after the payment of this charge on capital borrowing is attributed to the employees who produced it, and may be divided among them equally or in proportion to their notional contribution to the enterprise on any agreed basis. Control over the enterprise is typically shared among the employees in a similar way, by giving them the right to appoint and discharge their managers.

But legal notions of co-operatives provide little indication of their internal organisation, and legal status plays almost no part in determining practices. This is borne out by the discrepancy between ICOM's definition of a common–ownership enterprise, as one which is wholly

The co-operative model

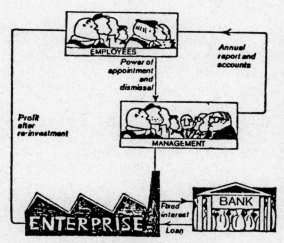

(Diagram from Hadden, 1972 : 396)

owned and controlled by those working in it, and the practices of its member companies. Scott Bader, for example, has the same form as a capitalist enterprise except that its profits are distributed to the workers. This conforms to a Conservative conception of co-operatives.

Many Conservatives see positive advantages in co-operatives

> so long as the workers who own the industry raise capital on the market and aim to produce a proper return on the capital, so long as they are subject to the same disciplines as anyone else running an industry
>
> *(K. Clarke, Conservative M.P., House of Commons,*
> *22/3/1977).*

Conservative opposition to the new worker co-operatives was due to the role of the state in financing the enterprises, rather than hostility towards co-operatives as such:

> we are certainly in favour of workers' co-operatives so long as they can be viable without continued support from public funds
>
> *(K. Clarke, Conservative M.P., House of Commons,*
> *22/3/1977).*

Conservatives see co-operatives and other schemes for workers' participation primarily as a way of improving industrial relations by increasing workers' involvement and responsibility, without really disturbing the balance of power within an enterprise. They expect co-operatives to replicate existing managerial practices and hope that this form of enterprise represents a threat to the traditional role of trade unions.

While the Conservative Party has viewed co-operatives from an industrial relations perspective, on the Left the issue has been taken up within the broader framework of debates on industrial democracy and workers' control. Co-operatives are seen by the broad Left as part of a socialist strategy, potentially providing both a model and a school for workers' self-management at the level of the enterprise and, ultimately, in the economy as a whole. They provide an opportunity for workers to demonstrate their capacity to run industry themselves.

Such trade union support as there has been for the new co-operatives has come largely from the shop stewards' active involvement in their very formation. Set up to save jobs, these co-operatives conformed to the traditional trade union role of fighting redundancies. Originating in a similar concern, backing for these co-operatives has also come from the left of the Labour Party. Central in promoting this strategy in the Labour Party has been the Institute for Workers' Control (IWC). Although it is a heterogeneous organisation, the IWC takes seriously the possibility of reforming the internal organisation of the enterprise while retaining capitalist relations of production.[5] A representative of the IWC has explained that by 'workers' control' they mean:

> The aggressive encroachment of trade unions on management powers in a capitalist framework
> *(Coates, 1965: 293).*[6]

This was how it saw the new wave of co-operatives.

With the benefit of hindsight it is clear that the idea of such an aggressive role for trade unions was a product of the 1960s, an optimistic period of near full employment. At that time it could be said that 'the pre-war disciplinary force of sustained unemployment running into millions is not an option' (Coates, 1965:189). But in the 1970s the changed economic and political climate forced trade unions onto the defensive. The new worker co-operatives were part of a defensive strategy rather than an aggressive one. The IWC has failed to take seriously the political and economic context when evaluating the strategic role of co-operatives. It has also been criticised for an inadequate analysis of the contradictory position of trade unions; a reluctance to confront explicitly the limits to reformist adjustment of the industrial control structure; and for skirting the issue of democracy within the trade union movement itself.[7] Rather than addressing these questions, the IWC has made a virtue of necessity by trying to draw out lessons for worker self-management from the establishment of 'defensive' co-operatives.

Opposition to co-operatives has come from the far Left, such as the Socialist Workers' Party and the International Marxist Group, and some sections of the labour movement. Ernest Mandel, one of the leaders of the Fourth International, opposes co-operatives on the grounds that genuine self-management, limited to individual factory units, is unrealisable in a capitalist economic system. He claims that:

> There have been many examples of workers' co-operatives that went wrong; there have been some that have 'succeeded'—in capitalist terms that is! All that they succeeded in, however, has been to transform themselves into profitable capitalist enterprises, operating in the same way as other capitalist firms
>
> *(Mandel, 1975:8).*

Although Mandel does support the struggle, in industry as a whole, for workers' control over the management of their factories as an anti-capitalist demand, he argues that workers in *individual co-operatives* are forced to accept the logic of rationalisation because competition imposes certain imperatives on the units of production.

On the far Left, workers' control is the central issue. Co-operatives are rejected as part of a more wholesale rejection of industrial democracy. The argument has been expressed thus:

> Most schemes for industrial democracy will involve an absorption of workers' representatives into capitalist forms of control, not a transcending of these: they will bring about the more effective integration of workers into existing economic and social relations, rather than produce any basic alteration in the capitalist system
>
> *(Clarke, 1977:375).*

Consistent with this is the same author's critique of the new worker co-operatives:

> Workers in isolated co-operatives remain at the mercy of market forces and government controls which destroy the possibility of substantial internal reform
>
> *(Clarke, 1977 : 372).*

This approach, which rejects industrial democracy schemes, including worker co-operatives, as incorporative, emphasises instead the need for strong shopfloor unionism and aggressive collective bargaining. It has found support among those sections of the labour movement which have adopted the model of industrial democracy put forward by Clegg (1960). According to Clegg, industrial democracy already exists in Britain, as long as there are strong trade unions maintaining a vigorous opposition to management. Any attempt, such as co-operatives represent, to extend workers' control into the realm of management threatens to destroy the very basis of industrial democracy—the autonomous trade unions.[8] Clegg's views have been echoed by the miners' leader Scargill (1978) who, in his inimitable way, declared that: 'Workers' control means in effect the castration of the trade union movement, means in effect a total collaboration as far as the working class is concerned.' The problem with this view is its failure to recognise the essential ambivalence of trade unionism. While ameliorating the conditions of workers' subordination to managerial control, unions do not and cannot contest the *fact* of this subordination. This process has been described as 'antagonistic co-operation': the constant interplay of conflictual and collaborative aspects of trade unionism (Hyman, 1974). The problem is posed even more sharply in the case of co-operatives where, in the absence of a conventional management structure, it is not clear how trade unions should organise to defend workers' interests. In so far as the trade union establishment seeks to control its membership it can only be an uneasy ally of the cause of workers' control or co-operatives.[9]

It emerges from this account that a polarisation of views
has developed on the Left. On the one hand, the position
adopted by the IWC and the Left of the Labour Party can be
described as the 'advance of labour' approach, which sees
industrial democracy, including co-operatives, as a strategy
for gradually eroding capital's power in the workplace by
extending worker participation. The logic of this position is
that even a partial abolition of certain capitalist forms points
the way forward for class struggle within the workplace.
On the other hand, the 'incorporation approach' of the far
Left sees industrial democracy as a strategy by capital to
incorporate labour and its shopfloor organisation into a
system of workplace decision-making, the outcome of
which is predetermined by the production relations of
society. It follows that in a capitalist market there is no space
for the reform of authority relations and work practices at
the enterprise level; this rules out the possibility of genuine
worker co-operatives.

But this polarisation of views is unproductive. In part, it
reflects the contradictory nature of the concept 'industrial
democracy' itself; its offer, at one and the same time, of
control of and yet submission to capital's domination of
work. Both the approaches outlined above suffer from a
failure to take account of the struggle between labour and
capital in shaping the precise form of the production
process.[10] The choice posed between working-class
autonomy and incorporation is a false one; some form of
co-existence and co-operation is always necessary between
capital and labour for capitalist production to be possible.
What is at issue is not whether such co-existence and co-
operation shall exist, but the *terms* of the co-existence and
co-operation between labour and capital.

Arguments about the principles of co-operatives and
industrial democracy inevitably reach the conclusion that
the political impact of co-operatives is an open question:
struggles over the control of the labour process are not in
themselves more or less significant than struggles over, say,
wage demands. Struggles over job control, for example, do
not necessarily lead to advances in class consciousness; they

may retain a conservative or even reactionary character. It depends on the general political situation and the traditions, consciousness and organisation of the particular workers concerned. But there has been little consideration of such factors in the context of co-operatives— the political consciousness and experience of the workers themselves has received scant attention. Certainly the significance of factors specific to women's experience is lost if the discussion is conducted at too abstract a level; failure to specify the sex of the workers effectively presumes a male subject. On the whole, the debate so far has been conducted at a general level, and has concerned the principles of workers' control.

Few detailed studies of the recent worker co-operatives have been undertaken, and hardly any have considered the precise nature of the democratised forms of organisation which have emerged.[11] In some co-operatives, organisational reforms have included the end of demarcation between jobs, the introduction of an egalitarian wages system, and a sharing of the technical knowledge of production. The possibility of such gains must be recognised, within a broad awareness of the limitations of co-operative enterprises. Clearly, none of the above reforms take place automatically when an enterprise becomes a co-operative— this change merely removes some of the constraints. It is therefore important to specify empirically the character of different co-operative forms. Some worker co-operatives have actually gone beyond the limited notion of workers' control as trade union representation in decision-making, to challenge the existing labour process and the division of labour. Even the social worth of the products themselves has come under scrutiny. Such co-operatives have implicitly questioned the conception of a democracy in the workplace based simply on the introduction of a formal structure of representation.[12]

Fakenham Enterprises was a co-operative set up by a small group of women in which, following an occupation, substantial attempts were made to democratise the workplace. Changes in the internal organisation of the factory towards more collective decision-making and the sharing of skills and work-tasks, and what became of these, will be explored in due course. These changes will be placed in the context of the relation between work experience and political consciousness. Meanwhile, the next chapter will begin to explore the economic history of the co-operative, reflecting the problems involved in setting up such an enterprise in a declining sector and an ailing firm.

TASS Journal Aug. 1972

3 Formation of the Fakenham Co-operative

On Tuesday 29 February 1972, Sexton, Son and Everard announced that it had called in a receiver. The news came as a shock, causing great anxiety and commotion in Norwich, the home of the firm. Yet it was 26 miles away, in the small market town of Fakenham, that the firm's action was to have its most dramatic effect.

This was the beginning of Fakenham Enterprises, the struggle of a group of determined women to establish a truly co-operative venture, which captured the public imagination and sympathy, but never received adequate support. However, before considering the events themselves we need to look briefly at the background in which they were set.

37

Fakenham

Fakenham is a small country town in Norfolk, with a population of under five thousand. Living there, surrounded by fields on all sides, is very much like living in a village—everyone knows everybody else and the community is tight-knit. The town seems very isolated, even though the nearest city, King's Lynn, is only 21 miles away, and Norwich a mere five miles further. Fakenham has become increasingly inaccessible over the past 20 years. The railway station was closed down as part of British Rail's 'rationalisation' policy during the 1950s and 1960s, while the bus service to Norwich is slow and infrequent. The bus journey to King's Lynn is no easier, taking an hour and operating at only hourly or two-hourly intervals. This lack of transport inevitably limits the possibility of seeking employment elsewhere.

Historically, Norfolk has been, and still is, an area of low pay; earnings here are nearly 8½ per cent below the national average.[1] Part of the explanation for this lies in the industrial structure of East Anglia, which has a high proportion of employees in agriculture—a relatively low-earnings industry—and hardly any high-earnings industry.[2]

In the Fakenham area itself, in the post-war period, despite a steady decline in the number of agricultural workers, 32 per cent of full-time employed males still worked in agriculture.[3] However, some manufacturing firms were attracted to the Fakenham area by the availability of labour, the proximity to raw materials and, in some cases, the fact that the parent firm was located in Norwich. Many of these firms regarded married women who had not previously been in employment as their most important source of labour.

Industries in Fakenham itself were few, and mostly small-scale. Before 1972, in addition to the shoe factory which was to become Fakenham Enterprises, there were a printing works, a construction company, a laundry, a clothing firm, and three food-processing plants. The largest, the printers Cox and Wyman, employed about 400 people, mostly skilled men. Brooke Bond Oxo (which has since closed), Jack Israel and Ross Foods used local agricultural products. These, together with the laundry and the clothing firm, provided the few women's jobs in the town. A few Fakenham people also worked at an American air base nearby, at Sculthorpe. Agriculture was the other employer of local people. Fakenham was surrounded by several large land-holdings, and some small self-sufficient farms.[4] Farm labourers worked, and lived, on these larger estates. (Most of the people who worked in Fakenham were council tenants.)

Jobs

The labour market in Fakenham was small and homogeneous enough for the women's knowledge of wages and employment conditions in the area to be fairly accurate. They had a realistic picture of the local labour market and had exhausted the limited employment opportunities that existed within it. While they knew they had little choice about the *type* of work, most women had no alternative but to get a job; for working-class families in Fakenham, the wife's wage was an essential part of the household income. Only two of the women at Fakenham Enterprises in the summer of 1975 were married to non-manual workers. One husband was a sales manager for the local branch of a Norwich bakery and the second was a security officer at Ross Foods— in 1975 they earned £50.00 and £55.00 respectively. The other husbands were all manual workers. Two worked at the American air base and earned as much as the non-manual workers; for the rest, take-home pay ranged between £27.00 and £45.00 per week. At that time low pay was defined by the Low Pay Unit as £40.00 per week.[5]

As a source of employment for women in Fakenham, the local onion factory was typical. In 1975, about 80 women were employed there at 69 p an hour—good pay for women in the town. Unions were not allowed into this factory. For their 69 p the women had to top and tail 120 lb of onions during the hour. A bonus of 3 p was awarded for every extra pound. 'You can't stop for a minute if you want to get 120 lb done,' complained Cindy, who got a job at the onion factory after leaving Fakenham Enterprises in August, 1975. In October 1975, I interviewed Cindy in her home; when I arrived she had just finished washing her hair to eliminate the smell of onions. I asked her how she was getting on at the factory: 'My hands have blisters from holding the knife; my eyes water when I get there, but then you get used to it. . . . Can you imagine sitting all day cutting onions? . . . It's so boring and monotonous. You go round the bend . . . start giving the onions names. I'd never do a job like that if there was anything else around.' With two school-age children to look after, Cindy worked part-time (9 a.m. to 3 p.m.), as did most of the women at the factory. They had to be at home when the children returned from school.

All the women with school-age and younger children mentioned the severe shortage of part-time jobs in Fakenham. Their choice of job was limited by their responsibility for child care. In these circumstances, the onion factory— providing part-time work and comparatively good pay rates— seemed an 'attractive' source of jobs. For these women, intrinsic job satisfaction was outside the realm of the possible; their experience of work had given them low expectations. I talked about jobs with Brenda A., Norfolk-born and bred, while she machined: 'I'd really like an interesting job— making things, like woodwork, with my hands, like children's toys. But I haven't got the brains and women like me with children don't get interesting jobs.' Brenda, who left school when she was 15 years old, had two school-age children. During her 16 years in Fakenham she had worked as a shop assistant, served in two canteens and delivered a bread round. She had twice lost her job because of closures— at the Brooke Bond factory and at the bread shop. Closures, however, were not the only problem, as Brenda explained: 'A friend of mine went for an office job and, as soon as she said she had a child, he refused her the job. What would he do if she was away because the child was sick or during the school holidays?'

Women's jobs in Fakenham, as in Britain generally, were concentrated in the lowest paid, least skilled sectors. Most of the women at Fakenham Enterprises had a history of unskilled factory work. Of all the jobs which they had previously held, 50 per cent were in food–processing plants or in clothing or shoe manufacture. (In Fakenham as a whole, 30 per cent of female employment was in food manufacture, and 27 per cent in clothing, leather and foot-wear.) Nearly all had experience as machinists or pro-duction line workers in the fruit and vegetable canneries. The rest had worked in typically female jobs, as shop assistants and waitresses, or in domestic service and agricultural work. Many women without a regular job did fruit and vegetable picking during the summer months when this type of work was available. Thus, before their jobs at Fakenham Enterprises, they had experienced consistently low paid, irregular and unpleasant work. Most of them had been laid off more than once during their working lives; the closing of Brooke Bond in 1974, for example, left many Fakenham women unemployed.

With little industry and a contracting agricultural labour market, high unemployment has been part of Fakenham's tradition, and lack of job security was still a recurring feature in these workers' lives.[6] Whatever happened at Cox and Wyman, in particular, affected everyone in Fakenham. Rumours of possible redundancies at the printing works produced an atmosphere of gravity and concern among Fakenham workers and their families; at that time, printing provided 35 per cent of male and 29 per cent of female employment.

The Shoe Factory

About fifty women were employed at the local shoe factory, which had been set up in 1964 and was housed in a small rented room, formerly a Congregational church. The parent company, Sexton, Son and Everard, was a family firm based in Norwich and had employed 1,750 operatives in its heyday. Set up towards the end of the nineteenth century, Sextons had pioneered mass-produced, machine-sewn shoes, reaching a peak of prosperity in the 1950s. Fakenham was the site of one of its satellite factories.

Making shoes is essentially a complex, labour-intensive, assembly process, involving many separate operations. There are four main departments, generally known as 'rooms', in a shoe factory: the 'clicking' and 'making' rooms, which are by tradition male rooms, and the 'closing' and 'shoe' rooms, which are traditionally female.[7] The clicking room, where the pieces which make up the shoe uppers are cut, is the first stage of production. An electrical press, operated by a clicker who places the press knife on the material, generally performs this task now. Traditionally the elite manual occupation in the shoe industry, clicking (cutting leather) is an almost exclusively male occupation; the skill involved is mainly that of handling leather and cutting it with discretion.

Then, in the predominantly female closing room, which is what the Fakenham factory was under Sextons, the pieces of shoe upper are assembled and fixed together, by a combination of stitching and adhesives, and any embellishments added. Within the wide variety of distinct work tasks carried out here, there are two basic types of job: a number of semi-skilled machining jobs, and tasks—unskilled and performed mainly by hand—preparatory or subsidiary to machining. The skills entailed in this work are speed, accuracy and dexterity. With many short and routine jobs, the division of labour in the closing room is extreme and it is usually in this department of the factory that there is most piecework.

The next stage in the process is the making room, where soles and heels are attached to the closed uppers. Although there is a range of possible methods of doing this, the most common is the cemented or 'stuck-on' method, using adhesives. Production is usually organised around a conveyor, passing the shoes between operators. The final stage is the shoe room—again a predominantly female department—where tasks include spraying, cleaning, inspection and packing.

The Fakenham factory performed only one of these tasks. Like Beccles, 18 miles from Norwich, where the other satellite factory was based, Fakenham provided a convenient source of cheap and ready labour, of which there was a shortage in Norwich itself. Both these factories functioned as 'closing' rooms, where workers used sewing machines to close shoe uppers. The machines were geared solely to this single stage of shoe manufacturing. Unable to complete the product, the Fakenham branch was totally dependent on the Norwich factory for its existence. The shoe uppers were delivered from Norwich pre-cut and returned there for completion. This state of dependency was exacerbated by the location of all administrative, managerial and marketing functions in Norwich; even machine repairs were carried out by Sexton's mechanics based in Norwich.

Factory Closure: the workers' response

In February 1972, 45 women were working in the Fakenham branch, both full-time and part-time. There was one supervisor and one quality controller; of the rest, most were machinists, while a few were benchworkers performing tasks unsuitable for machine-work. Because the management was based at the head office in Norwich and rarely visited Fakenham, the supervisor was a person of no small importance in the actual running of the factory. Though given little formal recognition by the central administration, she represented the only form of management on the premises. In 1972, this job was held by Nancy, an Irish woman who had come to Fakenham in 1947. She had worked for Sextons at Fakenham since the branch opened and was paid £25 a week for running the place. Although money was no longer a pressing need for Nancy and her husband, a construction worker, the job was important to her.

Nancy was responsible for co-ordinating the delivery of pre-cut leather to the factory and for the organisation and distribution of work within it. This was a straightforward task, as the technical division of labour within the factory was fairly rudimentary. In principle it was also part of Nancy's job to control the speed of the work and minimise differences of pace between machinists, but effectively piecework rates were the management incentive to ensure fast production.

The quality controller was a Polish woman called Natalia. She and her husband, an engineering worker, had lived in Fakenham since 1950, having come to England after the Second World War; they had two married sons. She had worked at the factory for eight years, checking the sewn shoe uppers for any faults and then packing them for delivery to Norwich. Whereas the machinists were paid by the piece, Natalia received the average rate of a fast machinist. Neither she nor Nancy ever used a sewing machine. As it transpired, these two women were to play a central part in the occupation of the Fakenham factory.

On the same afternoon as Sextons announced that it had called in a Receiver, Roger Spiller, divisional officer for ASTMS (Association of Scientific, Technical and Managerial Staffs) informed the *Eastern Evening News* that half to two-thirds of the staff were to be made redundant immediately. The newspaper reported that he was hoping to organise an occupation of the Norwich factory and raise sufficient capital for the firm to continue: 'We are determined to show that the employees are capable of running the factory profitably.' Later that day, the ASTMS Committee were arranging with NUFLAT (National Union of Footwear, Leather and Allied Trades) for a meeting of all Sextons workers to be held the following day. [See Appendix B on the Trade Union.] That evening, the ASTMS footwear branch, which had 50 members working at Sextons in a supervisory capacity, was to meet. 'In the meantime,' said Spiller, 'we shall see that nothing moves out of the factory.' He went on to say: 'We have been faced with this sort of problem before within the union, particularly at Fisher–Bendix, and that has stayed open . . . we would certainly consider a work-in at Sextons in the same way as we did at Fisher–Bendix.'

The president of NUFLAT, to which most of the workers belonged, affirmed that the closing of Sextons 'would be a tragedy for the Norwich industry and for the city . . . it would obviously be very difficult for the shoe trade to absorb anything like 700 operatives'.

On Wednesday, 1 March, 1972, the employees of Sextons met at St. Andrew's Hall in Norwich. This meeting of several hundred workers passed a six-point resolution — almost unanimously (the vote was 646–6) — giving their action committee the power to order the following:

(a) the occupation of the Norwich factory;
(b) to refuse to allow machinery to be moved out;
(c) to refuse to allow leather, boots or shoes to be removed from the factory;
(d) to take orders from their elected representatives;
(e) to refuse redundancy notices;
(f) to operate a 24-hour picket at the factory.

The local paper was quick to convey the men's sense of desperation. Leaving the factory at the end of the day, 49-year-old time-keeper, Jack Lamb, was reported as saying that he had been at Sextons all his working life and there would be no hope of getting another job. Lamb's wife also worked at Sextons and they were living in one of the firm's flats. The Lambs' total family income was in jeopardy. 'I think we shall try to have a work-in like at Upper Clyde. It's the only alternative,' she said.

Spiller announced that they would indeed occupy the factory unless assurances about the future of the company were forthcoming by Saturday. The next day, notices terminating their employment were received by the 700 Norwich workers. These were returned unopened the following Monday, on the advice of Michael Cooper — a spokesman for the joint ASTMS–NUFLAT union committee. The Receiver confirmed that he was giving the workers the requisite notice under their contracts of employment. This would vary from 1 to 8 weeks; nobody was being dismissed at once. He announced, moreover, that an offer had been made for the purchase of the business, which was being considered.

It was announced on 8 March that Mr. Jack Taubman, a property developer and manufacturer, had negotiated an agreement with the Receiver that ensured the continuation of Sextons as a shoe factory in Norwich. All the Sextons assets would be transferred and an estimated 500 out of the 700 jobs would be saved. During talks the day before, Taubman had been assured by the joint ASTMS–NUFLAT union committee of their agreement, as well as that of the works staff. Michael Cooper, union spokesman, said they now had the basis for a new company and it was his wish for everyone to pull together.

The 45 Fakenham workers were not included in these negotiations. They had continued to work normally while awaiting news of their fate. On 3 March, Nancy had been reported as saying that the women supported the ASTMS–NUFLAT action committee and would follow any action taken by it. Although the women had previously expressed fears of being forgotten, they were reassured by a visit from a union representative.

During the next fortnight, the new company, called Sexton Shoes Ltd, was formed with 423 employees—thus making 275 workers redundant. The Fakenham factory was to close at the end of the month; representatives of ASTMS and NUFLAT accepted the position. The first 30 Fakenham women were to lose their jobs at the factory on 17 March, although some women had already left. Brooke Bond Oxo offered to employ about 12 women, while Cox and Wyman announced that it could not take on anyone. This left most of the women with no hope of finding alternative employment. That day, approximately 40 women demonstrated outside the factory; much of their resentment was levelled at the trade unions, NUFLAT and ASTMS. Their feelings were expressed on a placard reading:

FORGOTTEN FACTORY SOLD OUT BY (NUFLAT) UNIONS (ASTMS) AND THE RECEIVER.

Some of these women had been at the factory since its opening eight years before. They all felt keenly the unfairness of the treatment meted out to their branch by Sextons, complaining about lack of consultation, loss of holiday pay, and the ineligibility of some younger workers for redundancy pay. This anger was to be quickly transformed into militant action.

This Factory is under Workers' Control

> Come and look around. Redundant workers answer
> to unemployment
> *(Placards on the factory door)*

The Fakenham workers met and decided to occupy the plant. Nancy conveyed the mood of the women:

> We are fighting for the right to work and will not give in. We will not be bought off and with the support of other workers we will win.

After attending the meeting, Roger Spiller told reporters that no materials would be removed from the factory until the women were satisfied that they were being fairly treated.[8] The women planned to stay in the factory 24 hours a day, continuing to work while there was any work to do. A new notice appeared on the factory door:

> THE PRICE FOR HARD WORK.
> REDUNDANCY.

Five women slept on the factory floor that night. Those with young children were not expected to take part in the occupation as this would cause undue hardship to their families. When management representatives tried to remove the machines, they were faced with barricaded doors. Food and bedding were brought to the factory next day, while the doors remained locked so that people could be screened before being allowed inside.

ASTMS officially recognised the work-in, but NUFLAT was not so willing. The following Monday, the women met the President of the Norwich NUFLAT branch and the branch secretary. They told the women that the Fakenham factory was now the property of the Receiver and warned them that they might be regarded as trespassers.[9] Showing scant regard for the women's efforts, and even less concern for their employment prospects, they maintained they could see no real point in the action. Natalia recalled that one of the NUFLAT officials told them 'not to be silly girls and go home'. As this attitude suggested, NUFLAT refused to officially recognise the occupation; although they were paying union out-of-work benefit, they refused to pay out strike benefit.

After several attempts to cut off the electricity and telephones, by the end of the first week of the occupation the Receiver had assured them that their power supply would be left intact. The previous management was no longer trying to remove machinery from the building, as the new owner had no immediate plans for the factory. Sextons were pursuing a policy of benign neglect towards the Fakenham factory; the new owner, a Mr. Glassman, said they could remain there, rent-free, provided they paid the power bills.

On Tuesday 5 April, the Fakenham women were joined by members of the Norfolk Women's Liberation Group in a demonstration outside NUFLAT's Norwich office. Carrying banners and leaflets, about 20 women picketed a union officials' meeting. The leaflets stated plainly that the Sexton workers' occupation was fighting for the right to work and continued:

> We are not a group of silly women. We are deadly serious. We have acted as trade unionists. Now the union should make our action official and give us full strike pay. Union officials should declare publicly that they fully support us.

NUFLAT officials agreed to reconsider their position. The very next day, they visited the factory, bringing a letter from the Union's National Executive Council. This urged the women not to approach other branches for financial support while the question of strike pay was pending. Outraged, Nancy declared that the union had denied them benefit, had refused to give them money from a shop-floor collection in a Norwich shoe factory and had asked the local trades council not to give financial aid. Individual NUFLAT members, ignoring the lack of official backing for the occupation, had themselves donated £88.

A decision on this contentious issue was finally reached and communicated to the women by the General Secretary of NUFLAT:

> The Union cannot officially condone the 'sit-in' which has been embarked upon, but it is prepared to continue that form of payment which has already been commenced, i.e. Union out-of-work benefit. [10]

This meant that the women would receive no strike pay, as their action was deemed unofficial. At that time, NUFLAT's female rate of out-of-work benefit was £1.00 a week for women who had been members of the union for one year, and £1.35 a week for members of three or more years' standing. Only Nancy was receiving more than this; being a member of ASTMS, which had supported the occupation, she received official strike pay.

The shoe union's policy resulted in considerable financial difficulty for the women—a situation that was aggravated by the withdrawal of unemployment benefit. This had been paid to five of the women, but was suspended on 6 April and then renewed the following day. Three days later it was again suspended. The reason given on both occasions was that 'the claimants have failed to prove that they are unemployed', and enquiries had to be made about any possible sources of payment to the women. Apparently, the local officials had difficulty deciding whether the women could be classified as available for work while occupying the factory. In response to this intransigence, eight of the women occupied the employment office, arguing that they were available for work but had been sent for unsuitable jobs. A hearing of their case was scheduled for 26 June— the delay effectively denied these women any financial assistance. They even wrote to the Department of Employment for government backing, but were firmly told that there was 'no possibility of government intervention'.

Although under severe pressure from both NUFLAT and the employment office, a fluctuating core of 12 women maintained their occupation for 18 weeks. Only some of those who abandoned the sit-in managed to find jobs during this period. Nine women were fortunate enough to find openings in a new Liptons supermarket in Fakenham. The rest were again relegated to, at best, irregular and unskilled employment.

Internal Transformation of the Factory

During the occupation, the atmosphere in the factory was transformed; the women organised themselves on a new collective basis. They participated equally in decision-making and all information about the factory was known to everyone. When she was asked about the internal organisation of the factory at this time, Nancy emphasised the increased democracy:

> The system that we have here is one by which any decision at all is fully discussed, talked round about. We look at it to see if it's beneficial to us—the whole lot of us—and we decide for or against it in that context.

These sentiments were echoed by Eileen:

> All decisions are made together whether it's over the phone, whether it's news or the post every morning—it's laid out for everyone to read. Every cheque is shown to everybody and listed so that we know all the money that comes in. . . . Everything is done together, every little thing.

Such direct participation was only possible because the group occupying the factory was very small. In addition, several of the women had been friends from the outset and loyalty to each other was an important motive for joining the occupation.

This sharing extended to the process of production itself. In contrast with the detailed division of labour that characterised the production process before the occupation, 'one person now makes one article and completes that article'. This was possible because the women, for the first time, were sharing their skills and knowledge. Using scraps of leather and suede, they turned to making leather skirts, handbags, jerkins and belts, to sell directly to Fakenham and Norwich markets. These scraps were remnants of the shoe production that had previously taken place in the factory, and were supplemented by donations from various sources. Income from sales was used to buy further materials, leaving little over to pay any wages: 'There is no regular payment whatsoever, for the simple reason that otherwise we couldn't buy the leather.'

Such money as was left after purchasing supplies was allocated equally or according to need. Although desperate for money, the women did not want, as Nancy said, 'somebody to just make a takeover bid for us and two years from now decide that the thing isn't a profitable concern and throw us out on the road again. We've had it so often.' Because of their previous employment experience, the women were suspicious that a new owner would have no scruples about introducing further redundancies. They wanted to be able instead to offer jobs to the women who had been forced to leave the factory, both because they could not afford to work without pay and because of pressure from disapproving husbands.

The women therefore planned to set up a co-operative, over which they would have full control and in which they could continue the practices they had developed during the occupation: 'We don't just want to revert to being creatures behind a machine with all the decisions being made by remote control.' Of these aims the women were sure, although it could not be said that they had a detailed plan for the organisational structure of the co-operative they envisaged. In fact, it was only later that the women defined their set-up as a co-operative at all.

The Wider Response

In sharp contrast to the shoe union's disregard for the Fakenham occupation, in other quarters interest grew rapidly. The national press picked up on the human interest value generated by a group of embattled country women defending their jobs. Apart from the standard television news coverage, several film crews also visited the factory. As a result of this extensive publicity, donations, sympathy notes and work orders poured into the factory throughout the occupation. A wide range of groups were excited by the action taken by the Fakenham women, and were eager to help. The intervention of feminist and left groups was important in terms of both financial and moral support. Feminist commitment to the occupation was explained by a member of a Norfolk Women's Liberation group:

> If men's jobs were involved there would probably have been a strike, but because they are women's jobs they are not counted. We want to defend the principle that women's jobs are very important. ... Although NUFLAT has mostly women members, it is run by men. The [Fakenham] women feel that the men are embarrassed about the whole thing.[11]

Although the women at the factory had not solicited support from the Women's Movement, and did not necessarily agree with 'all the images projected by it', they nonetheless welcomed this help. Many local feminist groups tried to find outlets for the leather goods being made, while the National Women's Liberation Conference, held during March in Manchester, raised a small sum of money for the factory.

Messages of support and donations were also received from the Fisher–Bendix factory at Kirkby in Lancashire. That April, workers there had held a successful three-week work-in to oppose redundancies threatened when the firm was taken over. In a spirit of solidarity with the smaller-scale Fakenham work-in, the 700 workers there guaranteed a financial contribution. Upper Clyde shipyards, site of the major contemporary workers' occupation, sent a further £250. In an effort to consolidate this support, the women invited workers who had been involved in such occupations around Britain to visit them. They held an Open Day at the factory in April, meeting various businessmen in the leather trade, as well as representatives from Upper Clyde ship-yards. This resulted in further publicity but little more.

The local response to the Fakenham occupation was quite different. Being a small community, most people in the town soon knew about it. The general reaction was one of surprise and amusement; it was not treated as a significant industrial action, a wholly unfamiliar idea, but as the whim of a bunch of troublesome women.[12] The local police did not take up an aggressive stance towards the occupation. As there was no management located in Fakenham, the women were not engaged in direct confrontation. The police were, therefore, not obliged to make any hostile intervention. On the contrary, concerned for the women's safety, some policemen were inclined to adopt a protective role towards them.

Launch of a Co-operative

'Well, girls, you can't carry on like this.'

Although the occupation was receiving national publicity and donations were considerable, financial backing on a much larger scale was needed to set up an independent business. The Fakenham women were looking for a backer to buy the factory from Glassman, who was willing to sell it for £11,000. Returning to the factory after a May Day meeting, the women found Derek Page, the then pro-spective Labour candidate for North-west Norfolk, waiting for them. 'Well, girls, you can't carry on like this', were his first words, as Natalia recalled. He had come to ask the women if they wanted him to contact Scott Bader on their behalf, as he thought they might help. The women agreed to this suggestion. As a result, on 15 May, representatives from Scott Bader had a meeting with workers' representatives from the factory and concerned union officials from ASTMS and NUFLAT, to discuss first steps towards legalising the work-in as a worker-owned, worker-run enterprise. Scott Bader's secretary wrote to the secretaries of ASTMS and NUFLAT asking them to help with a loan or a bank guarantee. He estimated the capital necessary to purchase equipment, premises and provide working capital at £20,000. The venture itself he saw as 'making industrial history where redundant workers are intending to work and not only that, but control their destiny'. He also wrote to Glassman offering to buy the factory.

The new company, entitled 'Fakenham Enterprises', was founded on 17 July, 1972, after two months of negotiations. It was financed by a loan of £2,500 from Scott Bader, which promised further funds if required. At the outset, Scott Bader envisaged that this initial loan would form only part of the seed capital. Other organisations had indicated their willingness to provide funds, but these never materialised. The women had no choice but to accept this offer, as nothing came of promises from alternative sponsors. The loan was insufficient to buy the old factory, so the women moved into rented premises over a garage nearby. The initial loan was to cover rent, the purchase of some of their old sewing-machines, and a few weeks' wages. It was agreed that all the women were to work a full 40-hour week and be paid at least the union minimum rate of £15.63 a week.

In accordance with ICOM policy, the workers were to have a stake in the ownership of the company through shares in it. A majority share-holding was to be retained by Scott Bader, while a minority holding was distributed between the nine women who had sustained the occupation. New employees were to receive a share of this minority holding after working in the factory for a period of six months. There was to be a Board of Directors, comprising three people (including a chairman) appointed by Scott Bader and three women elected by the Fakenham workers. Nancy was appointed as Managing Director and her co-directors were Eileen and Marice.

The co-operative was launched in a spirit of optimism. Two weeks after its formation it reported to ICOM that: 'a lot of offers of contract work' had come in for the shoe uppers and leather goods produced during the occupation, and 'strenuous efforts' were being made to harden these up.[13] The impression at the time was that the extensive publicity for the new firm would generate a substantial number of orders, bank loans would follow and 'generally the situation looks very hopeful'. As it transpired, this optimism was without foundation.

Thus, Fakenham Enterprises was established under the patronage of Scott Bader and ICOM. The legal composition of the company was left entirely to Scott Bader to formulate according to ICOM policy. Although this policy demands a form of control that is based on ownership, it was not supposed 'to offer one precise formula to suit all industries and all sizes of firm'. It would appear to allow the women a great deal of control over the actual internal organisation of 'their' factory. But things were not as simple as that.

While the women had a general notion of control through open discussion of, and consensus on, all decisions taken, they had no clear ideas on the exact form of company organisation they wished to adopt. This, combined with their dependence on Scott Bader and outside business expertise, meant that they were in a weak position to resist ICOM philosophy and practice. During the occupation the women at Fakenham had developed a highly democratic way of working. Although ICOM approved of this in principle, differences were to emerge over what was involved in a 'practical' form of organisation. The paternalistic conception of a co-operative, espoused by Scott Bader, was to have considerable impact on the development of Fakenham Enterprises.

Susan Shapiro

4 Profitability—the Immediate Priority?

It is one thing to set up a co-operative. It is quite another to turn it into a viable economic unit. Fakenham Enterprises had problems in finding adequate finance, a marketable product and competent management. While these are common in any small business, the last—managerial skills—is a special problem for co-operatives. In addition, a co-operative may be concerned to transform and sustain an alternative set of working practices and internal organisation in a hostile or indifferent world. All these problems are made much worse when, as in the case of Fakenham Enterprises, immediate and major problems of survival have to be faced.

Fakenham had been closed down by Sextons because it

was an unprofitable satellite unit. Although the enterprise's new autonomy enabled the women to go into production of any sort of leather goods, their work remained predominantly in the shoe trade where their experience lay. So it is most fruitful to consider its viability as a shoe-producing factory.

Throughout its existence, Fakenham Enterprises trod an uneasy path between doing 'labour-only' contracts and producing its own commodities. Before the occupation the factory had been doing sub-contract work for other manufacturers as well as the routine work for Sextons. In neither case did it manufacture a complete product for sale on the market. Rather, the factory was engaged in only one part of the process of shoe production—'closing'—the raw material being delivered pre-cut from Sextons. The co-operative failed to alter this basis for the relationship of the enterprise to the market.

The Struggle for Survival

Since the Second World War, and especially during the 1970s, the British footwear industry has been marked by slow growth and a relative decline. It is characterised by intense competition between a large number of firms in a diminishing or at best slowly growing home market. Competition has been further intensified by the sharp increase in imports from low wage competitors (see Appendix A).

Despite this gloomy background, it was not a foregone conclusion that Fakenham Enterprises would fail. In 1974, thirty women were employed there. But this did not mean that the firm was too small to survive. Two-thirds of all establishments in the footwear industry in 1972 employed fewer than 100 workers and 82 per cent employed fewer than 200 (Census of Production). Establishments of the size of Fakenham Enterprises accounted for 7.6 per cent of the number of plants in the industry in 1972. In terms of size, Fakenham Enterprises was potentially viable (see Appendix A).

Finding Finance

The co-operative was, however, set up with wholly inadequate finance. When the formation of the new enterprise
was planned, it was estimated that the capital required,
including working capital, was of the order of £20,000. As it
turned out, Fakenham Enterprises Limited was set up with
nowhere near this sum. It had financial backing from Scott
Bader, which had allocated a £2,500 unsecured loan at 6 per
cent interest for an unlimited period, as well as approximately £1,000 from other sources. The enterprise continued
to be heavily dependent on Scott Bader finance.

Initially, Scott Bader had envisaged that its loan would be
only *part* of the capital. Given its earlier estimates of capital
requirements, which seem to have been realistic, it must
have been clear to Scott Bader that the co-operative would

Table 1   Loans to Fakenham Enterprises from Scott Bader

Date	Amount
12.7.1972	£1,000
29.8.1972	£1,500
December 1972	£1,000
13.2.1973	£645
10.5.1973	£2,500
17.8.1973	£1,300
2.11.1973	£500
15.11.1973	£2,000
21.2.1974	£1,020
28.2.1974	£614
15.3.1974	£581
27.3.1974	£1,782
Total:	£14,445
Interest:	£1,309
Total amount owed to Scott Bader at 1.4.1974	£15,754

be undercapitalised and would therefore face crippling obstacles in developing its own products. This helps to account for Scott Bader's feeling that the firm's source of production lay primarily in sub-contract work—that is, labour-only contracts. Throughout its involvement with the factory, Scott Bader advised the women to concentrate on this type of work.

It is not surprising that, undercapitalised as it was, Fakenham required continuous subsidising by Scott Bader. (Details of the payments made are shown in Table 1.) Although the co-operative started out with plenty of offers of suitable contract work, it soon became clear that it was running at a loss. Initially, the women were engaged on contract work for shoe firms which had been their customers before the occupation. They also continued to manufacture the leather goods and garments which they had learnt to produce during the occupation. While the possibility of contracts for other types of work did arise, Fakenham did not have the specialised machinery and skills necessary to take these on. Nancy explained the problem as follows:

> We didn't like to have to go back to shoes. But we had to have some kind of contract work to bring in the bread and butter and provide continuity in production. We took what we thought were reasonable contracts, but we ended up getting a whole avalanche of shoes which we couldn't hope to complete in time. It wasn't economic for the companies to send them down in quantities we could cope with
>
> (*The Guardian—June 1973*).

During its first six months, therefore, the co-operative was faced with a severe shortage of continuous work. The situation was alleviated in November 1972 by the Envopak contract. This contract—for plastic postal bags used by government departments and banks—provided a continuous supply of work throughout the following year. For machining 500–600 bags a week, Envopak guaranteed Fakenham an income of £300.00 per week; by June 1973, the bags made up more than 80 per cent of the co-operative's output.

The women were aware that being so heavily dependent on a single customer had its risks, but they had little choice. The Envopak contract seemed the best available. As it turned out, it was not a profitable contract and Fakenham ran at a loss throughout the year. An explanation of this was later provided by a Scott Bader adviser, sent in to assess the profitability of the Envopak work:

> ... Fakenham have been competing with a cottage industry (where overheads are non-existent) and it seems have been required to complete the tail ends of batch lots. These have usually been required in a hurry so that the maximum number of operators have been put on the work and as soon as they get near to achieving an economical standard the batch gets completed, they are switched to a different product and have to start all over again.

Affirming the destructive effects of this pattern, one of the women recalled 1973 as the year when:

> Envopak were absolutely throttling us ... Every week you'd get a different sort of bag. We never stuck on the same product so we could never build up our speed. It might be six months since you'd had that bag before and you're back to square one.

To cover the losses on Envopak, the firm once again turned to shoe contracts. By early 1974, these had displaced the Envopak work as the staple product and for the first time Fakenham Enterprises broke even. This marked the beginning of a period of relative success during 1974.

The contract that made this possible and provided the firm with stable work for that year was supplied by Pell Footwear—an old customer of Sextons. In the first quarter of 1974, the co-operative made a profit of about £500.00, despite the impact of the 3-day week. By May 1974 Fakenham's financial position was healthy enough for a 5 per cent wage increase, although wages remained slightly below union rates.

Delighted that there was no longer a shortage of work,

the Board decided in February 1974 that the firm's main problem was a shortage of labour. Pell itself recruited more labour for Fakenham, provided a generator to cope with power difficulties during the 3-day week and offered to second a full-time manager to the co-operative for six months to oversee the Pell contract. The central role which Pell had come to play in Fakenham's livelihood is illustrated by these direct interventions in the firm's business decisions. While the contract was destined to end after a year, it did enable the enterprise to operate and even expand without external finance. But the enterprise's underlying weakness, its continuing dependence on contract work, remained. To anyone considering the factory then, as a small unit doing shoe upper closing for a large Norwich shoe company, the similarities with its former situation would have been only too clear. It was totally dependent on one supplier of work and was as vulnerable as it had been when Sextons collapsed in 1972.

By Christmas 1974, Fakenham Enterprises was employing around 30 women at wages of 59 p an hour. Having 'stood on their own feet' for about eight months, the women were naively confident. One of the worker–directors recalled this period as the only problem-free one in the co-operative's existence:

> We were working for Pells and Shingler and Thetford, and we were making money. Not a lot, we weren't any opposition to Charlie Clore [head of British Shoe Corporation], but there was always that little bit to put in the bank … we really congratulated ourselves that we didn't have any outside help, and it was going.

Unfortunately, their confidence was based on a lack of information about the current state of the shoe industry.

A Takeover Bid

The general economic recession and the continuing slump in the shoe trade were to compound the difficulties at

Fakenham. Early in 1975, shoe contracts were becoming increasingly difficult to obtain. Most factories in Norwich and Northampton—the centres on which Fakenham relied—were working short time. These circumstances laid bare the firm's vulnerability. Nancy understood the situation only too well: 'Naturally if they have any work, they keep it for their own people and don't put it out to contract, so we suffer more than their workers.' Regretting Fakenham's concentration on shoe upper production, she blamed the Scott Bader directors for the fact that the co-operative's fate was now so closely tied to that of the shoe industry.

The Pell contract, which had paid best, was soon phased out. Pells itself was short of work and therefore had cut back drastically the work being sent to Fakenham.[1] Shingler and Thetford was taken over by the British Shoe Corporation (BSC) and subsequently failed to renew its contract with Fakenham. By March 1975, the co-operative was desperate for work and money; it was at this point that Shingler and Thetford put in a take over bid for Fakenham. In an approach to the Industry Minister, Nancy wrote that:

> ....after a spell of doing quite well financially, the bottom seems to have dropped out of the shoe market, and there are mass redundancies in Norwich ... we are faced with the prospect of being left with only one main customer, i.e. Shingler and Thetford, which are part of BSC. They have made advances to us about our being taken over by them ...
> It will be such a crying shame if after three years we are forced to go back to square one and become just a subsidiary of the Clore empire.

She asked for between £5,000 and £10,000 'to conduct a feasibility study and a market study' as well as to produce a range of samples so that the firm could enter the clothes market. The Department of Industry refused to help because Fakenham Enterprises was not sufficiently important to the economy to warrant a grant.[2]

Meanwhile, far from supporting the women in their attempts to remain an independent enterprise, Scott Bader set about calculating an appropriate price for Fakenham Enterprises.[3] Resisting these pressures, the women voted unanimously to reject the take over offer; the co-operative survived, with wages cut to £10 per week. Whether the women would have continued to resist the take over bid is uncertain, as Shingler and Thetford withdrew the offer. It was hesitant about acquiring the enterprise because of the distance between Fakenham and Norwich, and because, as the Managing Director put it, the Fakenham workforce had 'too independent a spirit'.

Fakenham Enterprises was, then, threatened with collapse and did indeed cease to operate less than a year after this research was completed. We have seen that the establishment of a co-operative at Fakenham did not fundamentally alter the factory's relationship to the market—it was still doing sub-contract work for the shoe trade. Previously it had been guaranteed continuous work by being a sub-unit of a larger Norwich shoe firm. The major change was that it was no longer guaranteed this continuous supply of work. Common ownership meant the women were now 'free' to seek contract work directly on the market or to produce marketable goods. They were unable to survive on labour-only contracts because of their irregularity and low profit margin. The alternative to which they aspired was to manufacture their own product, but they never acquired the capital, the managerial or the production skills to realise this aim.

Managing a Co-operative

The economic problems of Fakenham Enterprises form part of the background to the conflicts that developed over how the co-operative should be run. But problems of finance and markets were made worse by a further problem that increased the women's vulnerability to pressure from outsiders who believed they knew how a business should be run. That problem was their own lack of management skills. The women themselves knew nothing of accounting, financial control, or marketing, for instance. This problem became particularly acute with the increased variety of contract work being offered to the new co-operative. Accurate costings in unfamiliar areas (not just shoes) were required, whereas no costings at all had previously been carried out in the factory due to its satellite status. Given the women's lack of experience and confidence in these skills, they naturally turned to the Scott Bader representatives for advice. The women expected them to provide help and expertise on the management side.

Tied Money

But Scott Bader's ideas were different from the women's. As characterised in Chapter 2, Scott Bader's system can best be described as one of worker participation in management, rather than self-management. It claims to operate through a representative structure, rather than practising direct democracy, because of Scott Bader's large size. However, at Fakenham Enterprises, a small firm, it made no attempt to institutionalise direct democracy. It is hard to see how it could have done, given that its conception of the role of managers is a strictly conventional one.[4]

Fakenham Enterprises was clearly a new departure for Scott Bader and the Industrial Common Ownership Movement. Hitherto, ICOM members had tended to be companies originally organised under a traditional management structure and later made over to the workers by the owners. Here it was faced with a group of women who had just gone through the experience of taking direct action on their own behalf and through this had gained a sense of confidence about controlling their own work situation.

Also, Fakenham was the first co-operative set up in response to redundancy with which Scott Bader became involved. Finally, the majority of members of all the other co-operatives Scott Bader supported were male. The women at Fakenham did not need to be convinced of the virtues of industrial democracy. They needed practical help: they lacked managerial, costing, selling and accountancy skills. But Scott Bader was prepared to offer these only in conjunction with a kind of co-operative significantly different from the women's conception. Until Scott Bader's withdrawal in 1974, the women had to contend with control exerted by the outside managers appointed by the Scott Bader directors, as well as by the directors themselves. Throughout its involvement with Fakenham, Scott Bader pressed the women to forego the co-operative practices of internal organisation which they had developed. According to Nancy, the results of Scott Bader's aid were:

> Fiascos. All the way along the line, from the first man Scott Bader gave us, who had been working with Rowens in Glasgow, went to Scott Bader and then came to us. He didn't have ... literally I suppose he didn't have the time because he was involved in his own book distribution project. He managed to give us two half days in a week which really wasn't any good at all. And he didn't understand ... the other man who came down from Scott Bader was a chemist by profession. He didn't have the vaguest idea what it was all about. He'd come down and have a look at some figures and on the basis of the figures he'd say, well, yes, this is what your recovery rate is, you've got to get in so much money per month, but at that it finished. He had no idea of telling us where to go to look for it.[5]

When Fakenham Enterprises was established, Scott Bader appointed two of their own directors, Brian Parkyn and Michael Campbell, who remained directors of the co-operative throughout the two years of Scott Bader's involvement. They were to give advice in their capacity as directors, as was Michael Ward in his capacity as company secretary. At the outset, Scott Bader employed Colin Johnson as part-time manager—he was to spend two half-days a week at the factory. He was experienced in a common-ownership and management having worked at Rowen Limited,[6] and was to spend three months helping

Table 2 Changes in the formal organisation and office holding at Fakenham Enterprises

	The co-operative is established July 1972	November–December 1972	May 1973	March 1974	May 1975	From May 1975 until the collapse of Fakenham Enterprises
Workers–directors	Nancy Eileen Marice	Nancy Pat elected Eileen and Marice leave	Nancy Anne elected to replace Pat	Nancy Anne	Nancy Anne leaves	Nancy remains the only worker–director
Managers	Colin Johnson appointed part-time manager— Leaves after 10 weeks		Richard Hicks appointed as part-time manager	Hicks dismissed Spreckley appointed as adviser	Spreckley leaves	
Scott Bader (outside) Directors	Brian Parkyn Michael Campbell		Parkyn Campbell	Scott Bader withdrawal: Parkyn and Campbell leave		

the women set up the business—charging £5.00 a day for his services.

In retrospect, it is clear that none of these men was really suited to the task; their experience was just not relevant to the special problems that faced the Fakenham firm. They knew nothing about the shoe industry or how to set up a small enterprise. Scott Bader was in the chemical industry and was a high-technology, capital-intensive firm, with a large workforce. It had been converted into a common-ownership firm 'from above' by its founder, Ernest Bader. Fakenham Enterprises produced a very different product for a different market; it was low-technology, labour-intensive, and had a small workforce. It had been created by the women themselves 'from below', and they had a much more positive commitment to working co-operatively than the Scott Bader workforce. The management techniques, knowledge and background required were of a different order. Parkyn and Campbell's only experience of a co-operative was of the Scott Bader organisation and it was this experience which they applied to Fakenham.

Johnson left after only ten weeks, during which Fakenham had no ongoing contract and was losing money on one-off orders. The earliest detailed report on Fakenham Enterprises, dated 10 March 1973, was written by Richard Hicks, who was to become a part-time manager. It is a clear statement of the problems the enterprise faced at that time. What follows is an abridged version of Hicks' report:

The worker-directors have no experience or knowledge of how to run a company. Financial expertise is non-existent, and the existing costing and pricing system is inaccurate and hopelessly out of date. There is no sales effort, beyond accepting orders from people who visit, and selling to stall holders in the local market. Office procedures are virtually non-existent, and no targets for production have been set or records kept of production achieved. The production effort of the Company has been dissipated by producing small quantities, and many special one-off orders for leather goods, shoes, etc., and often selling these below cost. It would appear that seldom, if ever, have proper prices, in writing, been agreed with the customer *before* production of the goods.

The striking thing about this report is that it could just as easily have been written to describe the situation at Fakenham Enterprises in the summer of 1975. The attempts, such as they were, to overcome these problems all failed—as we shall see.

Collective Working

As pointed out in Chapter 3, before the occupation, the factory at Fakenham had been entirely controlled from Norwich. Despite being physically cut off from Norwich, where all decisions were made and from where all materials were dispatched, this unit had very little autonomy. Being the sole representative of management based at Fakenham, Nancy supervised the women and ensured the smooth running of the unit. Work conditions and rules were, however, laid down in Norwich, so that Nancy's authority extended to the enforcement of these rules and no further. Payment was by piece-rates and this was the main way of maintaining the speed of the machinists.[7] This form of payment encouraged competition amongst the machinists, creating a tense atmosphere in the factory. All the workers were glued to their machines for most of the day.

All this was radically transformed during the occupation. As described earlier, the women who took part worked together and pooled all their earnings. At that time, Nancy's position as figurehead was just that; she had little special authority. After the co-operative was established in 1972, the women worked a 40-hour week for £15.63—their union minimum rate. At Sextons, the machinists had earned £18 to £25 a week on individual bonus schemes. But, according to Nancy, 'that's a cut-throat situation where everyone is grabbing to get a little bit more than the rest. We've rejected that' (*The Guardian—June, 1973*).

Brenda started working at Fakenham Enterprises two weeks after it was set up. This is how she, as a novice, described what it was like to work there at that time:

> When I came to the factory, just after the takeover, we used to work here all day and then go home and cook supper and then come back and work here from 8 to 10 p.m. for nothing. Only a few of us—Nancy, Edna, Pat, Natalia, Anne and me. ... We didn't need a lot of meetings then because you always knew what was going on, because it was fresh, the factory was starting fresh. Whenever they had a meeting and they wanted wage cuts, everybody's hand went up and they all worked ever so hard and nobody ever bickered, not really bickered. And you knew they wanted to work until 10 o'clock at night, they would all volunteer to come back ... There was a strong, nice feeling for the factory.

Although the Scott Bader representatives saw themselves as pioneers of industrial democracy, it was the women themselves who introduced concrete changes at Fakenham Enterprises. They insisted on carrying over into the co-operative practices that they had instituted during the occupation. The former piece-wage was replaced by a time-wage and all the workers (including the directors) were to get the same rate of pay. They hoped that there would be no rigid specialisation of tasks, and that skills would be shared. Smoking and talking were permitted during work hours and the radio was often playing. Any disputes within the workforce were to be settled (if necessary) by majority vote at open meetings, which were to be held weekly. It would be hard to think of a more 'democratic' framework for a small worker–controlled enterprise.

The initial involvement of Scott Bader did not completely change these practices. Early in 1973, the main source of Fakenham's work became the Envopak contract. Although the factory continued to run at a loss and was dependent on repeated injections of Scott Bader capital, there was a continuous supply of work. It seemed to the women that the factory was running fairly smoothly. The co-operative was still quite new and the women formed a fairly cohesive group. During an interview in February 1973, when she was asked if she thought the factory was more efficient since the women had taken it over, Nancy replied:

> Yes. It may not look like it to people who come in, who are used to seeing workers with their heads down all the time. You stop for five minutes. You can make it up again AND be more happy and relaxed. Some people think they have got to chain you down even when you are drinking coffee, and that you've got to have the chain gang atmosphere around you
>
> *(Libertarian Struggle—February 1973)*.

In the early days of the co-operative, everybody's job had been interchangeable. However, with the introduction of the Envopak contract, the organisation of production had changed somewhat.

> If we have some contract work it's a little bit different because the things we are making are more specialised, and you have to spread them out a bit. One girl will do one operation and another will do the next operation, but they will earn the same money
>
> *(Ibid., Nancy)*.

There was still no salary structure or wage differential. Everyone earned the same wage, irrespective of their skills

> In the early stages I think maybe some of the best machinists resented it a bit, because they could do perhaps three times as much as the younger girls who hadn't the experience. But they realise now that they have a responsibility to those inexperienced girls, the same way that the inexperienced girls have a responsibility to try. For everybody's sake, not just for her sake because it's adding 25p bonus to her wages. To try without gluing your nose to the machine again, and not having time to live or breathe
>
> *(Ibid., Nancy)*.

The hours that people worked were also fairly flexible. According to Edna, the shop steward, sick notes were only necessary in order to claim union benefit. Otherwise,

> we know she's off sick, so that's that. Nobody stays off sick unless they have to.
>
> (Ibid., Edna).

But pressure on the women to abandon their collective practices soon began to build up. Covering Fakenham Enterprises' mounting losses throughout 1973, Scott Bader was pressing for it to become economically viable as quickly as possible. At the Annual General Meeting, Parkyn (a Scott Bader-appointed Director) urged the women to:

> Achieve profitability quite single-mindedly without confusing this with the ideals of common-ownership. As soon as the concern is able to pay its way without financial assistance from us we naturally earnestly hope that it can become a common-ownership concern but no-one should be under any illusions concerning the immediate priorities.

The women themselves, realising the need for management expertise, asked the directors to appoint a full-time manager. They did not want someone with a casual interest in the firm, like Colin Johnson. But neither did they want someone who would merely take over and run the factory for them, as in a conventional company. They wanted a manager who would help them learn how to run their own factory efficiently, while retaining the changes they had instituted.

A New Boss

Richard Hicks, a furniture manufacturer from Kings Lynn, was a regular visitor to the factory in the early months of 1973. Hicks' company had recently been declared bankrupt, and he stumbled across the co-operative while pursuing the possibility of manufacturing children's leather clothes. He had been using outworkers for the manufacture of other leather goods but considered that Fakenham 'has the facility and skills under one roof that could provide goods to a realistic quality and price, thus benefiting the Company and myself'. Scott Bader officially appointed Hicks as part-time manager of Fakenham Enterprises on 1 May 1973—and he remained until the women refused to employ him any longer in March 1974. His salary was £1,000 per annum, plus 10 per cent commission on new business introduced.

In retrospect, it is hard to understand why the Scott Bader representatives thought that he would be a suitable manager.[8] He had no interest in co-operatives as such, and he had turned up at the factory because he saw it as a good business proposition. However, he was interested in the job and he was a local man. According to Anne, a worker-director, Scott Bader hired Hicks after they had failed to get an Envopak manager. The women did not want Hicks, but Scott Bader 'would put anyone in if they could get rid of the responsibility ... we needed a manager then, so what do they do! They go to our biggest customer [Envopak] who is throttling us and ask them for one of their men to come in and run the place. *We* weren't consulted!'.

Hicks suggested the following company reorganisation:

> A Board of Directors should be appointed, including existing employees, co-opted so as to keep the employees informed of the Company's policies, but *having no executive authority in running the company*. There should be a working managing-director [Hicks] responsible to the Board for the running of the company
> *(Hicks' report on Fakenham Enterprises—10 March 1973.* My emphasis).

Parkyn, on behalf of Scott Bader, accepted Hicks' suggestions for the structure of the company without any consultation with the workers or their elected directors. Hicks clearly wanted complete authority and Parkyn made no attempt to safeguard the women against the manager exerting 'over-much control'.[9]

From the beginning, Hicks got on badly with the women.[10] According to Hicks' view of a co-operative, it was the manager's, i.e. his, job to run the factory on behalf of the employees. After a month, Hicks expressed his approach as follows:

> 'What I've tried to do,' he said, 'is to create a situation where they've wanted to have a board of directors to run the business for them, and they've come round to this now. As shareholders they have the right to appoint the board, but there is no reason why anyone except the two women they've just elected on to the board, Nancy and Ann, together with the two Scott Bader representatives, should know completely the facts of the company. The co-owners are only employees and shareholders—not the management. Co-ownership is non-political because the shareholders invest their work and not cash'
>
> *(The Guardian—June, 1973).*

Hicks encouraged the women to hold meetings to discuss the company's operations at fortnightly intervals, instead of weekly, reporting to the board that:

> Co-ownership appears to have meant discussion at any time between all the employees of any problem which has arisen, generally in working hours, therefore lessening the production and adding to the overheads. This has now been stopped. Discussions take place during tea breaks or out of hours
>
> *(Manager's report—10 March, 1973).*

In advocating solutions to Fakenham's economic problems, Hicks took no account of the women's system of internal organisation. His solutions were those suited to a conventional firm and not to a co-operative of the kind operating at Fakenham. They took basically three forms:

(a) the introduction of time sheets;
(b) the introduction of some form of payment in accordance with productivity;
(c) redundancies.

Hicks stated that the key to profitability lay in the accurate recording of times 'to account for every minute of every worker's day', coupled with:

> Either an incentive or a payment by results for the work achieved. It is my opinion, though this may not be supported by the directors, that the speed of output in certain parts of the factory has slowed down very considerably and that there are machinists who are not earning their wages. Time sheets alone will prove this and it will then be up to the operatives concerned to increase their productivity or be either dismissed or take a lower wage
> *(Manager's report by Hicks—17 October 1973)*.

From what has been said in this chapter so far, it is clear that these measures would meet with resistance from the women. Had Hicks spent more time actually in the factory, he might have had more success in implementing his proposals. As it was, the women agreed to fill out time sheets but never, in fact, did so. Not only did he make no attempt to teach them management skills, but he tried to discourage their attempts to organise the enterprise themselves. An illustration of this was the way the accounts were kept.

During Colin Johnson's stay, an accountant had been appointed to teach one of the women book-keeping. Pat, who had taken part in the occupation, learnt how to do the accounts and continued to do them after Johnson had left. According to Anne, Pat kept the books quite well. 'You could look at the books then and know the financial state. . . . Everything was itemised down to the last 2p. Weekly accounts were properly kept, petty cash and everything.' This meant, in practice, that information about the financial state of the enterprise was accessible to all the women. Pat told me that she used to pin financial reports on the wall of the factory in those days.

Then Richard Hicks was appointed as manager. He took over the job of keeping the books, as Anne describes:

> He'd always had money all his life . . . 'never mind the expense, just get it' sort of attitude, whereas we've always

counted our pennies . . . it rankled a bit. We couldn't spend money the way he wanted to . . . we didn't have it to spend. He was willing to go thousands of pounds into debt sort of thing. Anyway, he said 'the books will have to be kept properly, I'll take them away to King's Lynn.' I said 'you can't do that, we need the books here.' 'Well, I'll look after them here.' He never touched them.

Hicks ordered Pat to stop doing the books.

So I realised after a few weeks that the books weren't getting done. So, at one of our sit-down meetings, we said: 'Mr. Hicks' . . . he had to have his full title. Everyone else was Anne, Mary . . . but he was Mr. Hicks . . . and he wanted to make that perfectly plain that nobody was to drop his title. Anyway, we tackled him at one of our meetings. 'The books aren't getting done and we think they should be done. If you won't do them then we think you should give them to somebody else who will do them.' Well, he didn't like the idea of the floor dictating to him. He was a typical manager of a conventional firm, you see. He didn't like anyone telling him what to do. 'Well,' he says, 'I'll have to take them away and get him [Hicks' accountant] to bring them up to date.' And he took the books away. . . . About three months later, we hadn't seen the books, we hadn't heard anything of them, people were asking us details we couldn't give them; we didn't have the books to give them. Well, when he eventually got sacked, the books weren't done at all . . . they were in a terrible state

(Anne).

By taking the books away, Hicks was taking information about the finances of the factory out of the women's hands. This information was a crucial resource that the women needed if they were to participate effectively in managing the factory. Hicks, however, thought that as manager he should exercise control over the employees. He was insensitive to the special problems which the co-operative posed. His class background and life experience were very different from the women's. He felt superior to them because of this class difference and also because they were women. In his relations with them, he was condescending. He took advantage of their vulnerability and tried to dominate them. By taking the books away, Hicks was trying to perpetuate their dependency on him. The women fought for the return of the company's books and to regain control. They grew to hate Hicks, but felt constrained to keep him on as manager because the Scott Bader directors had appointed him. They were afraid that Scott Bader would put them into liquidation if they insisted that Hicks leave.[11]

Exit Scott Bader

Hicks did not secure any profitable contracts for the co-operative. He had been hired to widen the product range and to improve costings and marketing. He proposed that the firm 'must look to a future in which they do not sell just their labour, but their own products'. While pursuing Envopak as their principal customer, they should try to develop a new market in leather clothing. The women themselves always wanted to manufacture their own goods, as they had done during the occupation:

> Remember when we finished that very first bag . . . we were all whooping and laughing, we were that excited. After years of doing nothing but shoe tops, specification work, this felt so *creative* . . . That evening we were rushing around, like maniacs, just admiring each other's handbags
>
> (*Sunday Times—August 1972*).

Hicks did try to develop four new products—suede clothes, leather handbags, bin chairs and leather belts. Some of these were already being produced—girls' skirts, jackets and belts. Hicks later boasted that he had won Fakenham Enterprises orders worth £950 for high quality children's clothes in pigskin suede which were sold in Harrods. He claimed that the Harrods work would establish Fakenham's economic viability. At that time, he reported to the Board that 'the principal hurdle in the future is the recruitment of extra labour' to produce these new lines; and the firm advertised for twelve more machinists. However, the co-operative continued to run at a loss throughout 1973 and it later emerged that it was not only the Envopak work that was unprofitable. The firm lost about £1,800 on the children's clothes for Harrods through, according to Nancy, 'mismanagement and a lot of other things'. It appears that Hicks personally was an agent for these clothes, thereby profiting as a middleman, as well as being paid as manager of Fakenham.

Scott Bader itself paid little more than lip service to diversification. The Scott Bader representatives insisted that the women do labour-only contracts—seeing this as the quickest way of achieving profitability. They did agree to the women producing their own lines, 'but only once a substantial amount of working capital had accrued'. It seems that Scott Bader never seriously considered itself providing the firm with the working capital it needed to develop its own products.

As well as failing to develop Fakenham's own product, Hicks also failed to manage the factory itself competently. He did not spend enough time there to keep an eye on things from day to day.[12] By October 1973, Hicks was under strong attack for incompetence from the Board. He laid the blame for the company's failure on low productivity. He wanted to avoid any adverse reflections on his own competence as a manager. Not only was Hicks uncon-cerned with imparting skills to the women, but he failed to exercise them himself. The Board's 'solution' was to make Nancy responsible for the day-to-day administration and control, leaving Hicks responsible for calculating costings. Although he was repeatedly asked by the Board to produce a complete breakdown of the financial situation, he failed to do even this. At its October meeting, the Board expressed concern that 'a closer relationship between Mr. Hicks and Fakenham Enterprises should be established' and concluded that a full-time manager was needed. In Ward's view, Hicks had demonstrated nothing except bad management over the previous months:

The factory is run on a day to day basis lurching from one
pay day to another—a situation that requires skilled management to survive
                    (*Ward's letter to Parkyn —19 October 1973*).

Nonetheless, Hicks was reappointed as general manager
with

Absolute authority to do whatever you deem necessary to
enable Fakenham Enterprises Ltd to be a profitable concern
as quickly as possible
                    (*Letter from Parkyn—14 November 1973*).

This action was taken on Parkyn's own initiative. He informed Hicks that Fakenham Enterprises really needed a
full-time manager and he hoped that Hicks could train one
of the women to gradually take on this job. He said that they
were looking for a full-time manager among the Scott
Bader staff, but

It is my strong personal conviction that if a General
Manager can be thrown up from one of the ladies at present
in Fakenham this will be a better and happier solution for all
concerned.

But the women had had enough. At a shop-floor meeting
held two days later, they passed a motion of no confidence
in Parkyn and Hicks. Further, the women called for Hicks
to be replaced by a full-time manager from Scott Bader or
ICOM. Parkyn and Campbell visited Fakenham a few days
later and it was decided that Hicks would not be reappointed. Nancy was to appoint one of the women as
manager so that her position as 'Chairman' could be seen as
quite separate. However, according to Nancy, no-one
wanted to take over from her at the Annual General
Meeting. This was not surprising, as the women lacked
both self-confidence and the skills involved. With Hicks
gone, Fakenham Enterprises was left without a manager.

Having covered Fakenham's debts for two years, Scott Bader had been waiting for an appropriate time to cut its losses and leave. Although it had spent around £15,000 by the end of its involvement, it had neither planned nor foreseen the final size of its financial commitment to the co-operative. Scott Bader's decision was finalised at a Board meeting on 28 March 1974. Returning all their shares, they agreed to loan Fakenham enough money to clear existing debts, leaving the co-operative with a total liability for loans, including interest, of £15,754 (see Appendix). Scott Bader made it clear that this was the end of its involvement with Fakenham. They subsequently agreed that the loan would be treated for the most part as interest-free and at no time was pressure exerted to obtain any repayments. Scott Bader's withdrawal was completed with the resignations of Brian Parkyn and Michael Campbell from the Board of Directors. A new board was elected— Nancy and Anne were to be on it for three years. David Spreckley, a founder of Landsman's Co. Ownership Ltd (an ICOM member-company), was appointed as adviser. Fakenham Enterprises was effectively thrown back on its own resources.

Conflict between Worker–Directors

So far in this account I have presented the women as if they were a cohesive group. I have done this in order to concentrate on outside interventions into the co-operative. But conflicts about management took place not only between the women and outsiders; they also involved divisions within the workplace. Whereas in the early days the women had formed a fairly cohesive group in opposition to Scott Bader's interventions, as the financial situation worsened, tensions between them grew. In particular, the relationship between the worker–directors, Nancy and Anne, deteriorated over the two years.

The first directors of Fakenham Enterprises were Nancy, Marice and Eileen. By Christmas, 1972, Marice and Eileen had left. (Marice left because of pregnancy and Eileen because of an argument with Nancy.) Pat was then director for a few months, until Anne was elected to replace her in May, 1973. For the following two years, Nancy and Anne were the internal co-directors of the co-operative — Nancy having been a director since the company's establishment.

As well as weekly meetings on the floor of all the workers, bi-monthly meetings were also held by the Board of Directors. These were attended by the outside directors, the worker–directors, the manager, and the company secretary (see Table 2 for details). These meetings, which were held off the premises in Ward's office, were the only direct contact that Scott Bader had with Fakenham. Parkyn and Campbell attended regularly and made decisions largely on the basis of managers' reports written for these occasions. The women directors often had to contest Hicks' interpretation of what was happening at the factory and what should be done about it. They did not have the skills to meet Hicks on his own terms — that is, to write complicated financial reports reflecting this or that weakness in the company. Further, the outside directors were inclined to treat Hicks' views more seriously. In the last instance, the worker–directors could be out-voted by the rest of the Board anyway.

Before the occupation, Nancy had been supervisor of the Fakenham branch of Sextons. Most of the orders the co-operative received when it was set up were from former customers of Sextons. They had grown accustomed to dealing with Nancy at that time and she had built up personal contacts with several of them. When they returned to do business with the new co-operative, they automatically treated her as if she still held a position of authority. This was partly because Nancy spent a lot of time in the office, where she had most access to information, often simply by virtue of answering the telephone.

Throughout her directorship, Anne remained for the most part at her machine and could therefore only find out what was happening by asking Nancy: 'and you can't keep asking, because you've got to get on with your work'

(Anne). Anne said that day-to-day decisions were being taken and most of the time she knew nothing about them and never got a say. However, major decisions were taken at Board meetings, and then there was 'only her and me against them' and so Nancy kept her informed.

Although these Board meetings functioned to unite Nancy and Anne, overall there was increasing tension between the two women. Their differing views on the sources and kinds of discipline appropriate to a co-operative were a continuing source of conflict. These differences were to do with the problems of operating a co-operative within an overall system defined by the organisation of private enterprise. How far this sytem set constraints on the form of authority relations within the Fakenham co-operative was not settled at the outset. The resulting informality left space for disagreement. Nancy did not recognise the need to introduce new methods of supervision and sanctions. Rather, she believed that, given the opportunity, the women would work hard of their own accord. Asked about the problem of ensuring that people worked hard in a co-operative, Nancy replied:

> Well, strictly speaking, I suppose if you stuck rigidly to the letter of the law, you could tell people what to do because they elect a Board of Directors who have to say this, that and the other. But I tend to stand aloof from that sort of thing because I think, I like to think, that they're implementing the thing themselves and making it work themselves.

Nancy was known to be extremely reluctant to consider the possibility that someone should be fired. When Anne would suggest it, Nancy's standard reply would be along the following lines:

> She should be given another chance. She's got a home and a family, she needs the money as much as the next person.

According to Nancy, Anne was a tough director:

> She was totally unfeeling and she'd sack anyone at the drop
> of a hat. Without giving them a chance. I don't think that's
> right. I don't think directors should have absolute control
> like that.

Anne, however, felt that stricter supervision was the only
way that the enterprise would ever become economically
self-sufficient. Although Anne was very critical of Hicks,
she felt that he did have some management expertise and
therefore sometimes wanted to follow his advice. She
actually voted with Hicks against Nancy over one particular
issue. This was over a proposal that redundancies were
necessary. Hicks calculated that with the existing flows of
money in and out, a cutback of four staff members was
needed for the firm to become viable. He made up a list of
the people he considered to be of least use to the factory and
gave it to the workforce to decide amongst themselves who
should go.
According to Anne:

> Nancy didn't like it. She had to put up with it because Hicks
> and I could outvote her, you see, it was the one time that a
> decision I agreed with could be seconded, against her. So we
> got rid of four people . . . well naturally it was dead wood
> that was going—we were getting rid of absolute rubbish.

Anne became increasingly frustrated at the co-operative
because of her exclusion from the decision-making process.
This resulted from Nancy's monopolisation of power within the factory. In Anne's view, Nancy was not running the
place properly, and yet she would not follow up any of
Anne's suggestions for improvements. Further, Anne felt
that Nancy was too lenient in her role as a director and that
some of the women were not pulling their weight. Anne
was acutely aware of how much work the other women
were doing, much more so than Nancy. Apart from Anne's
general outlook being more pragmatic than Nancy's, there
were two specific reasons for Anne's greater awareness. As

a machinist, she sat amongst the women all day and could
observe them working; also, because she was a fast and
competent worker, she did extra work to make up for the
slower machinists.

Anne grew resentful that Nancy would not exercise
stricter supervision. Worse, Nancy would refuse to support
Anne when Anne attempted to exert some kind of control
herself, as this story illustrates:

> One woman was systematically robbing our firm for
> months. She'd shout out how many hours she'd done per
> day. She'd been working seven hours for some time and
> then she changed. She was getting a lift, so she could work
> the extra time and then the lift failed. ... But she was still
> shouting out seven. ... It came to my ears that she was
> shouting seven and she was only working five hours. It had
> been going on for months ... So, by this time, everybody is
> involved. Nancy goes to the particular person, and says:
> 'Did you realise that you're giving in the wrong hours?'
> 'Am I Nancy?' 'Yes, you keep saying seven and you're only
> here five.' 'oh, I'd forgotten about that. I keep shouting
> seven automatically from when I was getting a lift'. 'Yeh, I
> thought it must be that. Well, if you'll remember in the
> future.' So a few minutes later, the woman goes over to her
> friend and says: 'What do you think, they've caught up with
> me at last. Bugger!'
>
> *(Anne).*

Anne was furious when it was revealed that the woman
had been robbing the firm for about six months. 'Girls
laughing behind their hands that she's been robbing us blind
... We're all supposed to be together.' When Anne told
Nancy to take immediate action to stop the woman, Nancy
refused to believe that anyone at the factory would do such a
thing. She even delayed making enquiries until Anne
pushed her to. This was made difficult for her, as Anne said:
'you always feel so bloody awful ... as if you've got a bad
mind'. Anne wanted the woman to be sacked, but Nancy
refused to take disciplinary action against her.

Anne's last fight with Nancy was about a take-over bid

for the firm in May 1975, which resulted in Anne's resignation. By that time, Anne was in favour of the firm being taken over:

> I was sick of it by then. .... The first year, the challenge was there. I put endless hours in. I'd come back and work until 10 p.m. at night . . . but then suddenly I realised that nothing would ever be any different and it didn't matter what I did. .... So, as a director, I was useless and then the rot set in.

By the time she left Fakenham Enterprises, Anne was totally disillusioned about the possibility of organising a factory co-operatively. When I asked her about it, she replied in a depressed tone:

> Each share-holder having a vote; it can't work because naturally the workers on the shop floor will outvote the management every time, and the management has the know-how. ... How many times has a bad decision to be taken and the unions have had to step in and call for a strike; but still, in the end the decision is taken because it's absolutely necessary and the unions have had to put up with it. Well, in a co-ownership, there's no strike, they just vote on it and it can't be done. And sometimes these things have got to be done to make the thing go.

Coming at a time when financial and managerial assistance had been finally withdrawn, Anne's departure left Nancy as the sole director of the co-operative. Which is not to say that this was the end of divisions between the women in the factory.

5 The Fakenham Women

It is now time to turn from the story of Fakenham Enter-prises to look in more detail at those most centrally involved — the Fakenham women themselves. When I arrived at the factory, in June 1975, there were twenty-two women working there. Figure 1 illustrates the physical layout of the factory and where people worked during my first few weeks there. There were seventeen machinists and they spent most of their day at their sewing machines. The other five women, including Nancy, could not machine. They sat at benches at the front and sides of the factory, doing a variety of non-machining jobs.

Nancy, Edna, Natalia, Pat, Brenda, Sue

The women who were the central figures in running the co-operative had all worked for Sextons and were the only

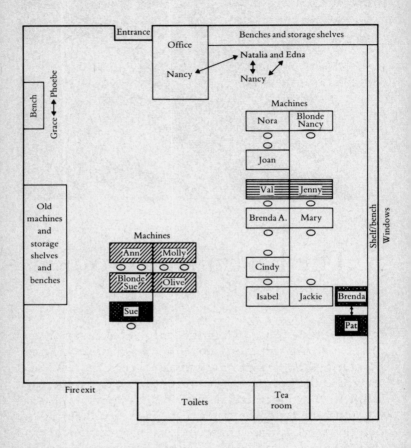

Figure 1 The layout of the factory

women still working at the Fakenham co-operative who had been involved in the occupation. All, that is, except Brenda, who started at the factory two weeks after the occupation. They all worked full-time (40-hour week, 8 a.m. to 4.45 p.m.), but they often worked late when it was necessary. Pat, Brenda and Sue were good machinists and would often stay back to finish off their own work and that which had been left unfinished by the women on the part-time shift. Nancy, Edna and Natalia could not machine. They organised the work — counting, packing, checking and assessing the work that had been done. These six women all spoke of Fakenham Enterprises as their own factory. They had played a leading role in the occupation and were all committed to working on a co-operative basis.

One of my initial impressions when I started work at Fakenham was that the factory was run from the front bench. Edna and Natalia sat there and Nancy often joined them when she was not in the office. These three women were all in their fifties and their children were financially independent of them. They had worked for Sextons for many years before the occupation. Sue and Pat were both young and lacking in confidence at the time of the sit-in, but had loyally followed the lead of the older women. Brenda also had a high commitment to the co-operative, and became integrated into this group soon after her arrival. These three women sat at the far end from the front bench, but were nevertheless part of this key group. Neither Sue, who was single, nor Pat, who was married, had children, unlike Brenda, who had three of school age.

From the outset, this 'core' of six women had given the impression that they were actually running the enterprise. This had happened partly by accident and partly by design. As a result of the continuity of their presence, and their tendency to leave the factory later than the other women each day, they had ample opportunity to build up an informal decision-making apparatus. This was part of their 'sacrifice'. They effectively drew a line around themselves by withholding the content and outcome of their discussions from the other women. The others saw them as

Table 3 The Fakenham Workforce

The women	Age (in 1975)	Single (S) or married (M)	Number of children (total)	School-age children	Children living at home and working	Children not living at home	When started work at F.E. [or Sextons, pre-1972]
Full-time workers							
Nancy	55	M	3	—	1	2	1961
Edna	52	M	1	—	—	1	1968
Natalia	52	M	2	—	—	2	1964
Pat	30	M	0	—	—	—	1971
Brenda	32	M	3	3	—	—	1972
Sue	21	S	0	—	—	—	1972
Jenny	17	S	0	—	—	—	1974
Valerie	17	S	0	—	—	—	1974
Phoebe	51	M	5	—	—	5	1974
Grace	48	M	0	—	—	—	1973

Part-time workers

Name	Age						Year
Olive	35	M	1	1		—	1973
Blonde Sue	20	M	3	3		—	1973
Ann	32	M	2	2		—	1974
Molly	41	M	0	—		—	1974
Cindy	31	M	2	2		—	1974
Brenda A.	35	M	2	2		—	1974
Nora	36	M	3	1	2	—	1974
Blonde Nancy	34	M	2	2		—	1973
Joan	42	M	3	1	2	—	1974
Jackie	23	M	2	2*		—	1973
Mary	38	M	1	1		—	1973
Isabel	57	M	0	—		—	1974

*One of Jackie's children reached school-age in the summer of 1975.

Table 4 Take–home pay of the Fakenham women's husbands, 1975

	Husband's average wage	Husband's occupation
Full-time Shift		
Nancy	£45	Construction worker
Edna	£30	Postman
Natalia	£40	Engineering worker
Pat	£27	Agricultural worker
Brenda	£45	Compositor
Phoebe	£40	Painter
Grace	£37	Agricultural worker
Part-time Shift		
Olive	£45	Compositor
Blonde Sue	£38	Fitter
Ann	£38	Welder
Molly	£40	T.V. repair man
Cindy	£55	Maintenance worker (USAF)
Brenda A.	£55	Security officer
Nora	£27	Agricultural worker
Blonde Nancy	£50	Sales manager
Joan	£55	Maintenance worker (USAF)
Jackie	£30	Casual jobs
Mary	£36	Dustman
Isabel	£45	Compositor

running the place and failed to realise that as often as not the information which appeared to be withheld was, in fact, non–existent.

Nancy

Nancy was born in Ireland in 1920 and came to England when she was single and in her twenties because she wanted to travel. Her husband, Michael, was also Irish and had left school at 14. They had settled in Fakenham 28 years ago because there were job opportunities for Michael. He had been a farm worker at first and a member of the agricultural workers union. He was now a construction worker and earned between £40 and £50 a week.[1] He worked long hours and usually at weekends as well. They had three children who all worked, one of whom lived at home and contributed to the family budget. The two daughters were professionally qualified teachers. The family lived in a council house—too small to accommodate them comfortably.

Except for Nancy, all the women at Fakenham Enterprises had left school at 14 or 15 years old. Nancy had been to university in Dublin and had an Honours degree in English. Her job history was, therefore, different from the other women's. In Ireland, she had worked as a school teacher and then a governess. Soon after arriving in England, she married and started working in factories, although often at a supervisory level. She stopped working for five years while her children were young and then returned to work to earn enough money to send them to college. She had enquired about a teaching job at the local school, but was told that she needed a modern foreign language; 'they don't count Gaelic, which was my foreign language'. However, she had never really enjoyed school teaching:

> I was never in love with teaching—formalised teaching—I
> wanted to teach in a different way. ... I enjoyed it for the
> contact with the kids but the syllabus thing put me off. You
> know you spout Shakespeare like a parrot or Chaucer . . .
> kids do it under pressure . . . the educational system needs
> revising.

Prior to working at Sextons, Nancy had organised a strike at her workplace in Wisbech. When she had discovered that Irish workers were paid less per hour than the other workers, she had organised a walk-out of the Irish workers. The next day they all went back to work and because of that Nancy quit the job. However, she applied to the Department of Employment on their behalf and the pay rise was granted.

She started work at Sextons in 1964. She joined NUFLAT and soon became shop steward. She held this position, and regularly attended union meetings, for about a year—gaining 'a lot of experience in what unions don't do!' Two years later, she became a supervisor and joined ASTMS. According to Nancy, the other supervisors at Sextons had pressured her to change her union membership from NUFLAT to ASTMS. She would not have joined it otherwise—'it's for white-collar people'.

Nancy played a central role in the Fakenham occupation and when I asked her if it would have occurred without her, she replied as follows: 'No, I don't think there was anybody else reckless enough to do it, to really defy the law and everything else.' It was Nancy who had suggested the idea to the Fakenham workers, having discussed it with the Norwich workers. But the idea of a sit-in had occurred to her before that:

> I think possibly the fact that the Clydeside workers had done it before we had and I was rather conversant with that and I thought—there's somebody making a stand against these redundancies. I think possibly that was at the back of my mind.

During the occupation, Nancy became something of a public figure. Newspapers have a tendency to focus on personalities, rather than on the collective nature of industrial action, and much of the publicity about Fakenham built her up as both a 'ring leader' and heroine of the sit-in. She travelled around the country giving talks about the occupation and trying to gain support. As a confident, articulate woman with a strong public presence, Nancy commanded respect and easily won people over. Although this publicity imposed great strains on her, she nevertheless enjoyed the public recognition.

Nancy was self-conscious about her leadership role; on the one hand, playing down her centrality and on the other, asserting it in the very way she talked about the other women:

> That's why I stay so much in the background and try to let them get on with it and make decisions themselves.

She stressed the importance of all the women working closely together and the strong relationships that had developed between them. And yet she said that she herself had no close friends at the factory:

> I don't have a confidant that's a woman. I seem to find it easier to talk to men—they have a more logical approach to problems. Women are too emotionally involved to see the problem clearly.

Nancy saw Fakenham Enterprises as a challenge and was determined to make it succeed:

> It represents an ideal I'd like to be instrumental in putting into practice. It's an ideal of how people should work together and what working conditions could be like given the right sort of circumstances. Life could be less of a rat-race and people could have the time to live and breathe.

She talked about the factory's informal atmosphere and how it made working conditions more tolerable.

> There's not a whole load of people walking around with white coats telling you what to do. You have to do it for yourself. It's character development too.

Nancy saw the co-operative as giving the women the opportunity to realise their potential, mainly by participating in collective decision-making—which Nancy considered the most important characteristic of the co-operative. At the outset, she had great hopes about what the enterprise might one day be. She described herself as an idealist and had great faith in the goodness of human nature:

> We should be able to work hard for a few days and then, if it's hot, shut the place up and all go off to the seaside for the day. People should be able to work when they like . . . but that's only possible in Utopia I suppose.

Edna

Edna was born in Fakenham in 1923 and had lived there most of her life. Her husband, Ted, was a postman, with take-home pay of around £30 a week. To earn this, he worked shifts: from 5 a.m. to 12.30 p.m. or from 12.30 p.m. to 9.15 a.m. They both left school at 14. Ted had been in a prisoner-of-war camp for five years. Soon after the war, while their son was young, he was made redundant and they had to live on unemployment benefit for six months. They both bitterly resented the government for not taking care of them after the war. They felt they had made personal sacrifices because of the war — such as leaving school early. 'I could have been a doctor' said Edna, 'if I hadn't left school at fourteen.' She had taken several evening courses since then: for instance, one in book-keeping and one TUC correspondence course on industrial relations and economic history. She was a strong and articulate woman with great self-confidence and determination.

Edna and Ted were both long-standing union members. Ted belonged to the Post Office Workers Union and, before that, to the G M W U. He supported the Post Office workers' strike in 1971 and for the twelve weeks that it lasted they lived on Edna's wages.[2] Edna was in favour of the strike and accompanied Ted to the local market place to hand out leaflets: 'You've got to because it's for my benefit as much as his.'

Edna began at Sextons in 1968, and worked full-time as a shoe checker. When I asked her why she had participated in the Fakenham occupation, she told me about her previous job history. 'I was fed up with being kicked around. I'd been made redundant twice before, remember.' Prior to working at Sextons, Edna was the manageress of a dry-cleaners and, before that, she had been the secretary of a chicken factory. Both the dry-cleaners and the chicken factory had closed down, leaving Edna redundant on both occasions. She had a domineering character and saw herself as having leadership qualities—her favourite job had been at the dry-cleaners, 'because I was my own boss and I ran the thing completely'. She then continued to talk about the occupation: 'We'd got nothing to lose; we'd lost our jobs and if we could save something . . .' Why, then, had she not just got another job? 'Another job! Christ! There were other jobs if you wanted that sort of job—but who wants to commune with a carrot all day.'[3]

After the occupation, Edna continued to work full-time at Fakenham Enterprises. During the occupation, she had taught herself to cut leather and she continued to do this job at the co-operative. She was the only cutter there and this job gave her a special status; cutting is traditionally a man's job in the shoe and clothing trades. Furthermore, she alone controlled her part in the labour process—no-one else could do her job. Cutting is a fairly skilled and creative job, and Edna found it satisfying. In general, she enjoyed being at work:

> I'd go bonkers if I stayed home all day for more than a few weeks . . . because housework isn't life. It's too dull for me. I like working because it makes me a bit independent and I can buy things for the house and [I could] educate my son.

Although they owned the small cottage in which they lived, Edna was not particularly house-proud and did not devote much time to housework. Her son was married and worked as a telephone engineer. She had encouraged him not to leave school early, as she had done.

Edna joined NUFLAT at Sextons in 1968, and was the shop steward of that union at Fakenham. She thought that

unions should foster the development of worker-partici-
pation:

> If I'm working in a place, I want to know where my sweat's
> going. Whether there's a fair return being put in for
> development. ... You see, the cake can be sliced very
> unevenly. I mean, why should a shareholder sitting at home
> get a bigger return out of my sweat than I'm getting.

She was, therefore, very enthusiastic about the possibility of
more factories becoming co-operatives:

> If it could be made to work, I think it's the answer to a lot of
> industrial problems . . . because people would feel involved
> in their work, and they would also feel that they're not
> classed as a load of morons who haven't got a brain to be
> consulted. ... And, I mean, people on the shop floor know
> their job, which people in the office don't. They know it in
> theory but theory is a lot different to putting it into practice.
> You've got to know both angles.

The Fakenham co-operative meant a great deal to Edna and
she thought that it *could* be the perfect place to work. Apart
from the extra freedom—

> You feel like it's a bit of you. Because what you put in, you
> should be able to take out, and if you don't put it in you can't
> take it out.

Edna had a fairly realistic attitude towards the daily problems of running a co-operative. She knew for certain that
several customers had come to the factory because they
knew how the place was run, and hoped to take advantage
of them. She thought that, as a co-operative, they were
particularly vulnerable, 'completely at everybody's mercy'.
However, in a wider sense, Edna felt both frustrated and
baffled by the persistent difficulties at Fakenham. Her
incomprehension was shared by the other women. An
obvious target for Edna's frustration were the workers

whom she characterised as 'not really caring' about the survival of the enterprise as a co-operative.

> The other drawback [of a co-operative] is that ideally you should be involved . . . well some feel involved and some don't. They don't want to be involved, they tell you straight. Well, you can't really work like that because you're making decisions for somebody else and then you get a call-back from them. . . . I don't agree with that, but they're not prepared to turn around and make their point of view.

The women Edna had in mind just wanted a job without any added responsibility and she resented their lack of commitment to the factory. These women all worked part-time and some were fairly new to the firm. However, Edna could not really explain why some were more committed than others:

> I don't know really whether the newer women . . . some of the women . . . understand what it's all about. The ideal situation when somebody comes in . . . is to have a couple of hours to explain what it's all about and what is expected of them. Because it's completely different from going in and working for a boss. . . . But you never get the time. . . . I mean, I'm working as well and if you can't explain things properly to people and let them ask questions back you can't really get it across.

Edna was referring to Olive and the three friends who sat with her, all part-time workers. They will be described shortly, and in the next chapter we shall see how this difference in involvement with the co-operative became the focus of much conflict within the factory.

Natalia

Natalia and her husband were Polish refugees who came to England in 1945. Natalia was 16 when the war broke out and spent the whole of it in a German labour-camp. They settled in Fakenham about 25 years ago. Natalia's husband described himself as an engineer, worked in the local food–machinery firm and earned roughly £40 a week. Like Nancy and Edna, Natalia was in her fifties and worked full–time. Her two sons were married and working—both having had further education. Natalia returned to work when the boys went away to boarding school, in order to help pay for their education. She said that she used to work to pay for household 'extras', as men's wages were low in the area. However, she increasingly felt that she had to work to make ends meet. 'We could just manage on his salary now that our children are independent, but we couldn't have enough even to go for a drive sometimes.' She enjoyed the company at work as well.

Natalia had started work at Sextons in 1964 and was the quality checker. She was involved in the initial stages of the occupation but had left soon after because she needed some money to complete her sons' education. She had returned to the co–operative six months later and had been there ever since. Nancy had asked her to return because they needed a checker. So she had done so, because she was a friend of Nancy's, and the pay was slightly better than she was getting. She had enjoyed working there for the first couple of years, but now said that she could not stand the strain any more. She wanted to leave but was afraid, both of losing her redundancy money, and of not finding another job. 'No–one would work here if there were jobs in town. Isn't it crazy to work for £10 a week. But it's better than nothing.' She added that many women workers had been getting the sack in Fakenham recently.

By the summer of 1975, Natalia felt that Nancy ought to realise that Fakenham Enterprises would never succeed: 'She should be realistic and close the factory and not extend the misery in a hopeless situation.' Natalia was usually tired and worried. She attributed much of her anxiety to the constant financial insecurity of working at the co–operative: 'I often can't sleep because I'm so worried about the factory.' She knew quite a lot about the factory's increasing debts, through her friendship with Nancy, and worried particularly about any legal repercussions that might ensue. The extent to which working at Fakenham Enterprises had soured her disposition, however, is hard to assess.

Pat

Pat was a shy, diffident woman of about 30. She and her husband, Lenny, had both lived near Fakenham all their lives and came from farm labouring families. Lenny was himself a farm labourer and earned between £25 and £30 a week. They lived in a tied cottage on the farm where Lenny worked, and, despite wanting children, had not had any. Pat had asthma and problems with her nerves, so she regularly took 'nerve tablets', which the local doctor prescribed. Ever since she had left school, Pat had worked full-time and she valued an interesting job. As Lenny said: 'Pat enjoys working at Fakenham Enterprises and that's the main thing.'

According to Pat, she took part in the sit–in primarily to save jobs: 'There was no work in Fakenham and it meant nearly 50 women out of work. That's a lot for Fakenham.' Lenny had supported her participation in the occupation and had helped out in various practical ways—such as bringing a television in. They were both in favour of co–operatives, and for Pat, 'There's more of an interest when you know how the factory is run and what's going on. Better than just going to work everyday.'

Pat had been a director of the enterprise from October 1972 until May 1973. During that time, she used to do the books, often in the evenings at home. She resigned from the firm soon after Anne Hunter was elected to replace her as director: 'I couldn't forgive the girls doing that to me after all the work I put in there.' About a year later, she returned on the understanding that she would just be an ordinary worker. But Nancy began to pressure her to become more involved. When Nancy asked her to do the books again, she refused, saying: 'Nancy should do them herself.' Pat did, however, answer the telephone and deal with business when Nancy was out and had asked her to do so.

Pat was very loyal to the Fakenham co-operative and had put in many extra unpaid hours over the years. She never complained about working so hard for so little pay:

> No, I don't mind. I don't want to see this place close. You go somewhere and people ask how Fakenham Enterprises is going and you want to say that it's going well. Anyway, I worked for free when it started.

Indeed, she was proud of the fact that she was not motivated primarily by the money:

> The girls here will work hard and pull their fingers out if they get good wages. They are only motivated by money, so they don't work hard here now. But I'm not just motivated by money.

Brenda

Pat's best friend at the factory was Brenda, although they were very different. Whereas Pat was extremely shy, Brenda was a real extrovert—lively and flirtatious. Like most of the women at the co-operative, Brenda had lived in Fakenham all her life, but her particular life history had made her into a tough, independent woman. She had married at 16, had her first child at 17 and a few years later separated from her husband. She brought up her three boys alone for seven years—going to work when the youngest was only nine months old: 'Maybe that's why I'm so hard.' Since then, she had done numerous part-time jobs. 'I've done lots of little jobs which lasted maybe one or two months or a few weeks.' A nine-month stint serving at the local fish-and-chip shop was her longest job before Fakenham Enterprises.

All three sons were now at school and she was the only woman with school-age children at the factory who worked full-time. When I asked her if working full-time had any effects on her children, she replied:

Well it just depends on the child. You know my children, they play out on the playing fields before they come home and then by the time I get home anyway they've just got changed and gone out to play. They never leave the garden. You know other people's children, they run the streets. In a case like that, I think that's wrong. You know, not to be here when they've come home. Depends on the type of child you've got, I think.

In 1973, she got married again to Ken, a compositor at Cox and Wyman, the Fakenham printers. He earned about £45 a week, and worked as a barman at the Conservative Club for four hours on Sundays. As they had a mortgage to pay off, they felt under considerable financial pressure. They had a far more active social life than anyone else at the co-operative and liked to go out, spend money, and enjoy themselves. They were both members of the Conservative Club and Ken was also a member of the Cox and Wyman Sports and Social Club. Pat and Brenda had a cheap pub-lunch at the Conservative Club every day and usually met Ken there. The club, which was just down the road from the factory, was the only political club in town, although Brenda and Pat stressed that 'it's really a social club'. Brenda particularly enjoyed the male company and the break from the factory which it provided. She sometimes worked there as a barmaid and it was her favourite job: 'Because you meet different people. I enjoy serving people and talking to all different varieties of people.' In fact, when she finally left Fakenham Enterprises, late in 1975, she took a part-time job at the Conservative Club.

Brenda started work at the co-operative two weeks after it was first set up. Like Pat, she often worked unpaid overtime at the factory over the years. It was always these women who finished off any machining not completed during the day and who assessed the feasibility of new contracts offered to the firm. Brenda talked about the positive aspects of working at Fakenham Enterprises:

Well, I enjoy the free and easy atmosphere. You know your job and you get on with it and when you've done your share you've done it and, you know, Nancy is easy enough to get on with if I want time off for the children or anything. Where other factories you have to clock in and out: if you're four minutes late you lose a quarter of an hour in the other factory.

However, for Brenda, working in the co-operative meant working harder than in a conventional factory and entailed more worries:

Now most people if they work in just a factory they clock on and off and that is finished, but at our place you are on call Saturdays, Sundays, night-times to come in, do this work, do that and every week you worry, you know, will you get paid for what you have done.

Brenda felt that some women did not do their share of the work, and this upset her:

... that gets you down. You can be trying to push all you want but the next person isn't pushing the same as you; well you're just lost. That's the thing I hate most.... If you worked in a normal factory, you have to reach a certain production, but in our factory if somebody didn't really want to do their share they don't do it.

This problem was exacerbated when several of the original group who had taken part in the occupation were replaced by new recruits:

When I first started there, that was for common ownership and everybody worked together for the same target, and then the people who done the sit-in—a lot of them left, the main people anyway and new people came, but they haven't got the same idea of common ownership, to them that's a job.

The experience of working at Fakenham Enterprises had convinced Brenda that co-operatives could never work on a large scale:

It's all right if there's some, say, six or seven of us, right, and then, say, they get a share. The people who join afterwards, they don't have as much say as those six or seven who are there the longest; because when you can build a factory up from seven and you can work up to fifty and if they're all going to be equal, you can never get fifty people to agree. They have to call meetings and say, now should we do this or should we do that, it's not on, you can't do it. That is where we have gone wrong. We should have, I mean even me joining straight after the sit-in and being there three years I wouldn't have disagreed if, say, the people who done the sit-in had a share and the most say in a factory, 'cos they earned it. But knowing how it is, people there six months, I don't really think they earned that share, and equal say in what other people had done for three years to keep it going. I don't think they should have the same say. You could never get everybody to agree.

Sue

Sue, who turned 21 during my stay at the factory, left school when she was 14. Being single, she lived with her parents. She had worked at Halmers, a small clothing firm in Fakenham, for three years before starting at Sextons. Although only 17 at the time, she had participated in the sit-in. It was the only machining job in Fakenham, she said, except Halmers—which she had hated:

I didn't want to go back to Halmers and I didn't fancy working in a food factory and we were all mates and we knew each other very well—so we all stuck together. Nancy and the other girls said we'd win, so I thought I'd stick with them.

She valued the freedom and friendly atmosphere at Fakenham Enterprises and identified with the factory:

That's your firm and you take out what you put in. With other factories, that's just a job.... It's more like a family business. You can have time off when you want it without worrying about it.

Jenny and Valerie, Grace and Phoebe

There were four other women at the factory who worked full-time. They all thought of Nancy as the 'boss', 'like in any other factory'. None of them felt involved in the factory's organisation and they played little part in determining the fate of the co-operative.

Jenny and Valerie had both been at the factory for about a year, since leaving school at 16. They worked as machinists, sat together and were friends. Both were living at home and contributing about £6 to their respective family budgets. Valerie was Brenda's sister, and was less shy and more vocal than Jenny, who thought that even though she had no say in what went on at the factory, other women sometimes did. Valerie was in favour of allowing workers a say in management: 'Because they have to do the work, so they should know better than the management whether they can do it or not.' According to Valerie, although Nancy made most decisions by herself: 'Everyone has a say [in decisions taken]—nothing can be passed without a majority vote.'

Grace and Phoebe both came to work at the firm in the previous year because 'it was the only job available'. Neither of them could machine, so they sat together and did 'bench-work'. Phoebe's five children were now financially independent of her, so she worked mainly for the 'company' and the 'extras'. Grace on the other hand, had no children and had always worked full-time. For 26 years, she had been the 'nanny' for the boss of the farm where her husband worked and where they lived. Her husband was not often at home because he worked all hours on the farm. She was very lonely and isolated on the farm. Her doctor had advised her to work full-time because of this, as well as regularly prescribing tranquillisers for her 'nerves'. Phoebe and Grace wanted a regular job and did not want to take on any responsibility. Common ownership meant no more to them than: no strict supervision, no clocking in, a relaxed atmosphere, and 'wondering if there is going to be any work in and whether I'm going to get a wage at the end of the week'.

Olive, Ann, Blonde Sue, Molly

Among the part-time women, there was a distinct group, consisting of four women who were fast and skilled machinists. They sat together in the centre of the floor, rather isolated from the other women except Sue, whose specialised machine was located near them. These women formed a friendship group and always left the factory together, at 3.30 p.m. sharp. With the exception of Molly, they all had school-age children and so left the factory punctually in order to meet their children after school. They also delivered their children to school before coming to work.

The most important aspect of a job to them was convenient hours. The part-time shift was specifically designed to fit in with school hours. During the school holidays, the women with children could have time off or bring their children into the factory. They worked in order to contribute to the family budget and clearly gave priority to their family roles. Molly, however, worked part-time because of 'bad nerves', which she saw as resulting from her inability to have the children she had so desperately wanted. She worked in order to forget about her problems—'for the company'.

Olive, Ann and Molly had all worked at the Sextons branch in Fakenham for several years, beginning in 1964. Olive and Ann had left to have children and Molly left because of a nervous breakdown. They had returned to work at the co-operative over a year ago, because it was then the only shoe factory in Fakenham. Sewing shoe-uppers was their favourite job. Thus, the enterprise had a dual appeal to them—a combination of convenient hours and a satisfying job.

These four workers appreciated that Fakenham Enterprises was a co-operative and thought that it could be a good place to work 'if it wasn't for bad management'. They had missed most of the period of Hicks' management and they meant by this that Nancy was to blame for the firm's problems. They complained of the continual uncertainty about wages, like most of the women. However, they identified this as the result of Nancy's failure to demand high enough profit margins from customers. Their solution would have been to hire someone 'to manage the place properly'. They supported the principle of everyone having a say in decisions, but claimed that Nancy made decisions on her own. Ann believed that: 'We should all get an equal say in the running of the factory, but we don't. Nancy makes most of the decisions without consulting anybody else.' None of them felt that they took part in decision-making; as Ann expressed it: 'I don't know any more here than I did at Sextons. Even when I speak at meetings, Nancy doesn't hear what she doesn't want to.' As they were experienced machinists, these women particularly resented Nancy ordering them about because 'Nancy knows nothing about machining—the manager should know how to do most of the jobs in the factory.'

Olive

Olive was the most articulate member of this group and often spoke on its behalf at meetings in the factory. Having left school at 15, she worked full-time for five years as a machinist at the local clothing firm before getting a job at Sextons. She left to have a child and returned to work when her daughter started school. She firmly believed that: 'Mothers should only work the hours that children are at school. You should be at home when the children come home from school.' During the school holidays, she either brought her daughter into the factory or left her with her mother-in-law. Olive would have had more children had it not been for her health. Her family always came first: 'I like home life—I have my family and I don't care about much else.' Olive's husband was a compositor at Cox and Wyman and earned £45 a week. So why did Olive work at all?

> I like the company and I like being independent of my husband. What I earn is mine—I don't have to take things out of the housekeeping money, for example, to buy a dress.

Even though Olive was not deeply involved in work, she felt that she had put a lot into the enterprise and said that she would hate to see the factory shut:

> Only a few of us could machine shoes and we taught the others and shared our skills and worked for low rates. We've all made sacrifices for this place.

It made a difference to her that the firm was a co-operative: 'I suppose I have the feeling at the back of my mind that that's our factory—that we're working for ourselves.' Further, it meant that:

> You're not under pressure to work like when you're working for piece-work rates—where it's all heads down and one against another ... you get a more relaxed atmosphere if you're all paid the same.

We shall see, however, that this view did not last. Olive said that she was enthusiastic about working for a co-operative and regretted that she did not have more time to get involved: 'If I worked more than part-time, I'd do both my jobs badly; that is, run my home and do my job.'

Cindy, Brenda A., Nora, Blonde Nancy, Joan, Jackie, Mary and Isabel

The remaining eight women, who worked part-time, sat at the machines to the right of the factory and enjoyed each other's company on the whole, but were not particularly close friends. According to one of them:

> The worst thing about this factory is the cliquishness of the people— there's a split in the factory between two groups of people.

She was referring to the disagreements that often occurred between the founder members and the women who sat with Olive. They did not see themselves as involved in such conflicts.

These eight women had all left school when they were 15 years old and had not done any training since. Isabel was the only really good machinist amongst them, having about twenty years' experience of various machining jobs. The skills of the others varied, ranging from those who had done a few years' machining at some time and were fairly competent, to the three women who had come to the factory as bench-hands. They had been put on machines only a few months previously and were still extremely slow.

Like the other part-timers, these women all rated convenient hours as the most important aspect of the job. With the exception of Isabel, they all had children at school. Isabel, aged 57, was older than the others and did not have any children. She worked mainly for the companionship, but got tired if she worked long hours and complained about the noise in the factory. The other women all said that the best feature of the firm was flexibility in the hours: 'No-one misses you if you take the day off', to go to the dentist, for example. Joan and Nora came to the co-operative in December 1974 after the factory they worked in laid off most of its workforce; this was the Brooke Bond Oxo plant in Fakenham, where they had packed vegetables on a moving belt, from 6 p.m. to 10 p.m. They had both liked the hours because they avoided the problem of school holidays.

In discussions about Fakenham Enterprises, the choice between taking school holidays off or bringing children into the factory was particularly stressed. Jackie had worked at

Fakenham for two years and said that the best thing about it was: 'that I could take Wayne. I took him all day for the two years I worked there. Nancy said it was O.K. So I didn't have to pay someone to look after Wayne.' Jackie badly needed the money, as her husband was employed rather irregularly. Some of the other women, however, worked for 'extras' and for 'a little bit of independence'. As one woman put it:

> It's nice not to have to rely on your husband the whole time. My husband works hard and I like to feel that I help out a bit . . . you feel that you can just buy say, a dress, and know it's your money. I spend most of it on the children.

Although perceptions of the enterprise as a co-operative varied a great deal, all the women remarked on the friendly, relaxed atmosphere there: 'It's like a home away from home. There's less tension than in other jobs.' Cindy agreed:

> I like the atmosphere. Well I know people bicker, but there isn't the strained atmosphere here like in some other places I've worked. You don't get the feeling you're being watched here. You're left to get on with your work and if you get on with it, nobody bothers you.

Cindy and Brenda A.

Cindy and Brenda A. were broadly typical of this group, although their husbands' pay was higher than the other women's. Cindy was 31 and had two children at school. Her husband had two jobs because they were paying off a mortgage. His day-time job was as an air-frame fitter at the U.S. Airbase at Sculthorpe. He earned £260 (gross) a month from this job and also had a seasonal evening job at Ross Foods. He worked there between 5.45 p.m. and 11.15 p.m. packing on the production line—for the extra earnings. Cindy said that she enjoyed going out to work:

Because when you're home all day on your own, there's no
stimulus. There's nothing. I see nobody except my
children—especially with the hours my husband works.
I'm not a great visitor of other people's homes. When you're
home, you miss the company and the constant activity.

Cindy thought that Fakenham Enterprises was not a
'true' co-operative:

Everyone has more freedom of speech than in another
factory. When you're at a meeting and talking, you feel
you're part of how the factory is run—but, the rest of the
time, I just felt that Nancy was like a manager in any other
factory.

Although she realised that bad organisation was a problem,
'some days there's a lot of work and some days there's
none', she saw the firm's main problem as being the fact that
'the girls aren't willing to work hard when we *do* have
work. They all fall to pieces.'

Brenda A. was 35 years old and had two children at
school. Her husband was a security officer at Ross Foods
and earned £55 a week. She came to Fakenham Enterprises
'because I heard they were lenient about school holidays'.
Like Joan and Nora, she had worked at Brooke Bond Oxo
until it closed down. She had served and washed up there in
the canteen, and now was the 'tea-lady' at the factory. She
had no idea what a co-operative was when I asked her and
just said that:

I've never been in such a lenient factory. You don't have to
work very hard and you get all the holidays you want.
Nancy isn't strict enough.

She thought of Nancy as the boss who made all the
decisions and of whom she had no right to ask questions and
demand information because, she said, she had not worked
there long enough: 'Nancy is very busy doing things and
can't just stop and answer questions. Anyway, it's none of
our business.' This remark was made when Brenda did not
know if she would get paid that particular week!

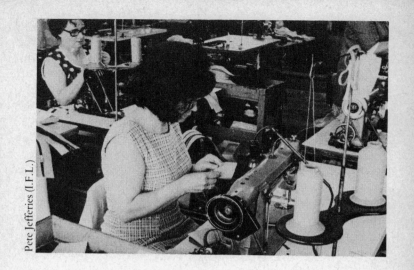

Pete Jefferies (I.F.L.)

6 Going It Alone

In the last chapter we met the Fakenham women. In the next two chapters I will look at their working lives, firstly in the factory and then, in the next chapter, outside it. This chapter will examine decision-making processes in the factory during the summer of 1975, when I was working there. In order to understand the major sources of conflict that took place, I will look in detail at one large contract, the 'K.' contract, on which the factory became dependent during that summer. Shortly before my arrival, David Spreckley, the last link with Scott Bader, resigned in protest at the women's refusal to accept a take over bid. Anne Hunter resigned over this issue too. Nancy was left as the only director. The women were now completely on their own.

We have seen that shoe contracts had become increasingly scarce during 1975. Both Pells and Shingler and

Thetford withdrew their contracts and for most of March and April the enterprise was desperate for work and on the point of bankruptcy. To survive this period, five of the original women worked for two weeks without pay doing odd bits of work. Then some work came in and the wage was set at a flat rate of £10.00 per week, regardless of the hours worked. When I arrived at the factory in May, 1975, therefore, work had been very scattered and irregular for the previous two months. Tension was high in the factory. Largely as a result of the widespread publicity the co-operative received during this crisis, a few small contracts arrived at the factory in May, as well as numerous orders from the women's movement. Wages were raised to 50 p an hour. With shoe work now virtually impossible to find in large quantities, the women were forced to use their skills on other types of work.

Embattled Women — The Public Response

In response to the co-operative's impending collapse, the press once again took up the Fakenham story—what could be better than women in struggle during International Women's Year! Several articles appeared during March and April; for example, *The Guardian* (3 April 1975) featured 'Fakenham ladies scurry to stop take-over'. Nancy appealed to the public for £1,000 to tide them over, and for 'any kind of contract in either the clothing or the shoe trade'. She told the press that all the women were desperate to resist a takeover.

Groups which had responded earlier to the occupation began again to take a more active interest. The ICOM organisation, as distinct from Scott Bader's direct participation via its directors, had been in contact with the enterprise throughout its existence. It now held a working weekend at Fakenham to which several members of other ICOM co-operatives came. The purpose was to help organise the factory and do general interior building work. There had never been an office at the factory—it was just open floor space—so they built one. This office area was to become identified as Nancy's domain and served to physically separate the women on the floor from the management area. This ICOM weekend was later remembered by many of the Fakenham women as the only time when they really felt part of ICOM.

A feminist who attended this working weekend as a member of the Sunderlandia Co-operative helped publicise Fakenham's crisis at the Socialist Feminist Conference held in London during March. As a result of this, several women from Cambridge—myself included—agreed to co-ordinate a Fakenham support group in East Anglia. It seemed obvious that feminists should support the only working women's co-operative factory in Britain. The conference passed a unanimous motion in support of the venture. Needing immediate help, Nancy had appealed for orders and donations. With shoe contracts completely unobtainable, she believed that their only hope was to break into the clothing industry and make their own products. As they had during the occupation of 1972, feminists again sent orders for leather goods to Fakenham. A Brighton feminist managed to galvanise the Co-operative Party into passing a unanimous motion at their annual conference to support Fakenham Enterprises and press their local societies to place orders.

Hundreds of orders, donations and letters of support reached Fakenham from all over the country. Women's groups, students' unions, trade unions, co-operative societies, retail outlets and marketing agencies made enquiries. The firm was, however, unable to take advantage of this goodwill because it could not provide accurate information on products and prices. In these circumstances, it was not clear what help was needed or what these groups could offer. The situation was chaotic when, along with Hilary Knight, another member of the Fakenham support group, I went to work at the factory in June. We spent our first fortnight there sending back nearly all the orders and deposits which had been received, mainly from feminists. It was simply not feasible for the women to manufacture a series of one–off orders; as one of them recalled:

> They ask for a waistcoat, we didn't have a pattern so we nip down the road for a size 38 pattern which is 50 p to start with. We were willing to have a go ... but the next order is for a size 32 and we haven't got anyone who's been in the trade long enough to alter the patterns. Down the road and another 50 p ... when it works you're only getting a few bob because there's been so much time spent on it. It was useless really.

From Crisis to Crisis

During my first month at the factory, the women were working on four separate contracts. Each was too small in itself to provide enough work for all the women in the factory for more than a few days. They were short-term contracts which had been brought to Fakenham because it was known that work could be done there quickly and cheaply. As with all the work that the factory took on, these contracts had materialised as a result of approaches from the customer, rather than having been sought out by the women themselves. The factories that usually did this work were temporarily overloaded and could not manage the orders they had to fulfil. Given the chronic shortage of work, the Fakenham women were ripe for exploitation and the businessmen knew it. One of them expressed interest in the special problems of co-operatives, but it seems this was a sham and always secondary to economic motives. Predictably, none of these contracts was profitable.

Fakenham Enterprises had no choice but to accept them. They were offered few others and the contracts did provide work for everyone in the factory. Two were straight-forward machining jobs which most of the machinists could manage. Speed, rather than skill, was required for these jobs. Eight of the part-timers and the two youngsters were allocated this work. The skilled machinists—Olive and her friends, plus Brenda, Pat and Sue—were working on an order for leather bomber-jackets. This order was for 72 jackets at £3.65 per jacket sewn. The order had come from London with the promise of a large order at a better rate of pay to follow, if the jackets were done well. As there was no-one at the factory who was an experienced leather-clothing machinist, it took the women a lot of time, patience and effort to learn how to machine jackets properly. Shortly after they had delivered the finished jackets to London, the customer telephoned to complain about the poor quality of their work. The order was not renewed and the customer may well have had no intention of commissioning a second order. As far as I know, they did not even receive payment for the work they had done. The fourth contract was for the uppers of evening shoes and entailed the knotting of silver straps. This was a bench job—that is, it required no machining—and so kept Grace and Phoebe occupied. Nancy and Natalia organised the work and Edna cut out leather bags and belts for the prepaid orders received from the women's movement.

On Tuesday 17 June, the three machining contracts had been completed. As there was no other work, during the morning the women gradually moved over to the benches to help Grace and Phoebe with the leather straps. The driver from Pells arrived from Norwich to collect the finished work and reported that the machinists at Pells factory were on short-time. There was a feeling of panic in the factory and rumours spread that more leather jackets were expected that Thursday. At mid-morning Nancy called a meeting, but not to discuss the overall situation. Rather, tasks had to be allocated. She turned the radio off and stood in the middle of the shopfloor. The machinists then switched off their machines and everyone sat silently in their places. Nancy announced that they had been promised more leather for bomber-jackets, which was supposed to arrive any day. She asked for a volunteer to learn book-keeping and stressed that it was their factory and they had to be prepared to learn new skills. Also, she asked for volunteers to attend a forthcoming ICOM weekend. Both these requests were met with silence. Then people started talking amongst themselves, roughly in the groups in which they sat. A lot of the discussion took the form of excuses offered for not having volunteered for the two jobs. Very few questions or comments were addressed to the meeting as a whole. As with most such meetings, this one ended informally when people started switching their machines back on.

Directly after the meeting, Nancy and I drove to Norwich. There was no work at the factory and we had not been paid for the work we had done. When we arrived in Norwich, we headed straight for Pells to collect the money owed to us. We then visited Florida Shoes, taking the samples that we had made up. They did not like the samples and said that they had no work for us. As Nancy rarely left the factory in search of work and we were desperate, this was a real blow. We returned to Fakenham in low spirits. In our absence, there had been discussion about some women staying away from work next day because of the lack of work. On their own initiative, a few women volunteered to stay away and told Nancy this as they left the factory.

The next day, there was still no work in the factory. Several women did not come in and those who did sat in friendship groups and tied the silver straps together. The bad news about the bomber-jacket contract was received by telephone that afternoon. Everyone was depressed and very worried about the prospect of not having any work and, consequently, no wages for the next week.·

Social Relationships Deteriorate

Clearly, the lack of orders was to take its toll on Nancy. My first impression on arriving at the co-operative had been that Nancy made all the decisions. However, after a few days of working there, I began to think that Nancy talked over decisions with Natalia and Edna, while they sat together at the front bench. Further, I noticed that these three women assumed they had the authority to order the other women around. When the contract for the bomber-jackets had been offered to the enterprise, for instance, Nancy had discussed it with Natalia and then had consulted Pat and Brenda about whether they could do the machining. Then, having decided to take on the contract, she had approached several machinists and chatted inform-ally with them about *how* the work for this contract could best be organised. Further, it was Natalia who talked to the representative of a shoe factory when Nancy was absent on one occasion. After he had left, she had discussed the possible contract with Edna. When Nancy was away from the factory, she usually asked Pat or me to answer the telephone. Nancy trusted Pat's loyalty and did not see her as any kind of threat. Apparently I was another obvious choice, as most of the women, including Pat, were shy and unconfident about handling phone-calls. I also bought a few note-pads and tried to institute a system for recording messages, but no-one took any notice.

The following week there was still hardly any work at the factory. Nancy reported that the bank had been reluctant to pay out their wages. Morale was extremely low. Nancy telephoned around and elicited some vague promises of work from London later that week. Most of the women continued to come to the factory that week anyway. There was growing discontent and many of them commented on hating to be idle. The lack of work in the factory was generally seen as a result of bad organisation and most of the hostility was, therefore, directed at Nancy. She was blamed for the fact that there was no work and received complaints from all parts of the factory. As the days went by, the groups of women in the areas into which they were physically divided increasingly took on the characteristics of tightly formed cliques. As Cindy observed:

> Have you noticed that there's three distinct groups in this factory.... We more or less decided to put our machines in these places.

Cindy was referring to her feeling that Olive and the

machinists who sat with her stuck together, as did Pat and Brenda. It was not so much that she felt a member of a particular group; rather, she felt excluded from these other groups. Olive's clique was particularly virulent in their discussion of what they viewed as Nancy's 'incompetent management'. They resented Nancy for making all the decisions and bossing them around. Likewise, Natalia and Edna did not escape their criticism. Olive accused them of doing very little work and yet being paid for the eight hours they spent in the factory.

I had been surprised to see Edna join that group of women for lunch, shortly after I started work at the factory. They usually brought a packed lunch and ate it at their machines, and I joined them. As I had suspected, Edna had approached them so that she, too, could deride Nancy. Edna was particularly angry about Nancy's intention to rehire a women who had quit the co-operative:

> Workers who have stuck the factory through the bad times should get the benefits and not those who leave and come back when things are better.

In fact things were worse, but Edna's statement reflects the way she felt. On such occasions, however, Edna's underlying complaint was that Nancy was the only director in the factory and there were supposed to be three. She was concerned that Fakenham's management should be genuinely *shared*. She complained specifically about Pat being authorised *by Nancy* to answer the telephone and that Nancy now did the books without reference to the other women. She suggested that they elect two more directors at the next meeting; this proposal fell on deaf ears. She then went on to complain about Nancy withholding information: 'When I ask her about what is going on, she tells me that I'll be told when I need to know something.' The lunchbreak finished with Olive upset and joking about quitting to go fruit picking. While she was aware of the tension in the factory, Nancy did not see this situation as one in which there was any element of choice. She asked

Nora where the rumours about her hiring more workers had originated and said that *she* would tell everyone if she decided to do this. She seemed upset by the gossip and claimed she could not understand why people did not ask her about things instead of gossiping. According to her, there were a few important decisions and then there was just the day-to-day running of the factory:

> There aren't many important decisions to make. The last important decision was to consider the recent take-over bid and on that issue everyone voted unanimously to refuse it.

The tension continued for nearly two weeks, at the end of which a Mr. K. of London offered a temporary solution to the work crisis in the form of a large contract for sewing skirts. Each week he would bring the cut material and take away the skirts sewn the previous week, paying a certain amount for each skirt and a contribution to overhead costs. While this contract eased the immediate economic crisis and prevented a serious breakdown in morale, it also generated its own problems and it is on these that the next section will concentrate.

Money and Time: division of the workforce

In the previous chapter, I described how the workforce at Fakenham Enterprises seemed to polarize around two distinct positions in the factory. There were the 'full-time' workers, who uniformly started work at 8.30 a.m. and were supposed to finish at 5.00 p.m.; and there were the 'part-timers', who started at 9.00 a.m. and finished at 3.30 p.m. (Both groups took a half-hour lunchbreak.) All wages were paid at the standard rate of 50 p per hour; the 'eight-hour' women were therefore drawing £20 a week, and the 'six-hour' women £15. The factory was only supposed to operate five days a week.

This distinction was not reflected by different *degrees* of 'commitment' to the enterprise, but by different *kinds* of 'commitment', which led the women in one position to openly criticise the commitment of women in the other.

The 'six-hour' group consisted mainly of women who had children of primary school age, whom they took to school before work and met afterwards. This specific 'commitment' to their children had prevented such women from taking part in the original occupation. But it also implied a specific 'commitment' to the co-operative, because this was the only kind of work in the area which allowed a woman either to time her periods of paid employment to coincide exactly with the duration of school terms, or alternatively to bring her small children into the workplace during school holidays. Jackie brought her pre-school age child, Wayne, into the factory every day.

The 'eight-hour' group included the six founding members of the co-operative, of whom only one had dependent children. These women were 'committed' to Fakenham Enterprises in a different way. They liked to place emphasis on their nominal 'ownership' of the company, and this was associated with a willingness to work *extra time without pay*. This 'sacrifice' seemed necessary because of the violent periodic fluctuations in the amount of work to be done: sometimes there was too much and a deadline to be met, and sometimes there was hardly any at all, and an insistence on being paid for mere presence in the factory would put further strain on the company finances. On the grounds of their sacrifice, these women would say that the six-hour group were 'less committed to the factory' because they 'only did it for the money'; there was a tendency to dismiss genuine constraints placed on the mothers of young children as consequences of their 'attitude'.

The K. contract brought this difference to a head in the summer of 1975, in a series of heated disputes between women of the two groups. Knowing full well that the women were desperate for work, K. baldly stated the terms on which he would offer them a contract. These were hopelessly unprofitable for the co-operative from the start. K. had a small factory in London, but mainly used homeworkers for labour.[1] He employed a driver who regularly collected work from these London homeworkers. He came to Fakenham because he thought it was a good business proposition; furthermore, his driver would only have to make a trip there once a week. He would treat the women as a collection of homeworkers who 'happened' to work under the same roof, while willing to pay a small contribution to the factory's overheads. The K. contract led to certain changes in the factory. It involved the introduction of machinery owned by K. into the factory and an agreement by the workforce to operate in teams working a full eight-hour day. The women were in no position to argue about the terms of the contract. Their only choice was *who* would work the eight-hour day.

It was only after accepting the contract that Nancy called a meeting to discuss it. She announced that K. wanted to train ten full-time machinists the following week and asked for volunteers. Emphasising its importance for the development of Fakenham Enterprises, Nancy pointed out that this was their first possibility of a long-term contract. All the machinists who usually worked full-time volunteered to work on the K. contract. Five more full-time workers were needed and there was heavy pressure from the full-time women on the others to volunteer. Nora, Brenda A., Joan, Blonde Nancy and Jackie put up their hands. They felt it was worth making sacrifices in a last effort to enable the enterprise to succeed. During the meeting, several people (including Nora) had made comments about this contract being the factory's last chance. They said they were so demoralised that they could not take another setback. The K. contract seemed to be the break they had been waiting for. No-one from Olive's section volunteered.

There was virtually no work to do all day, and I spent that afternoon sitting with Olive, Blonde Sue, Ann and Molly. They were very worried that they would be forced to work an eight-hour day and they emphasized the difficulties which this would cause, feeling that they had to justify their position both to themselves and to each other. Olive,

Blonde Sue and Ann insisted that they needed to pick their children up after school and, therefore, could not work an eight-hour day. Molly, who had no children, said that a full-time job would be a great strain on her health. This issue brought sharply into focus their long-standing resentment of the founding members. At the end of the day, Nancy approached the foursome for a chat which soon turned into an argument. Under pressure to work an eight-hour day, they responded by arguing for the introduction of piece-work rates—knowing this was anathema to Nancy.

These arguments about piece-work rates had recurred periodically during the co-operative's existence. The women who had taken part in the sit-in had consistently opposed any form of wage differentials. In the early stages, they had worked for equal pay, regardless of hours and productivity. It was only later that they had changed over to payment by the hour. It had always been Nancy's position that piece-work rates went against all co-operative principles. Piece-work, or payment by results, involves the organisation and measurement of tasks to such an extent that all initiative on the part of the worker is eliminated.[2] It imposes a competitive self-discipline rather than providing the basis for collective self-management and as such is inimical to the ideals of co-operation. That this position was supported by Brenda, Pat and Sue was more surprising, as they were skilled machinists. A piece-wage system would have been of practical advantage to them. It would have reduced the necessity for their personal 'sacrifice' by rationalizing the relation between input and output in a situation rendered chaotic by the lack of proper calculation within the enterprise. However, given the overriding problem of efficient management, a piece-wage system would have been more difficult to administer fairly. Be that as it may, this was not the argument used by the original full-timers to defend the time-wage system, nor did they seem concerned to reduce the extent of their own 'sacrifice' to the company. Instead, they used an argument familiar amongst workers who are *not* in nominal control of the means of production, viz.

> Piece-work goes against everything we stand for—it's
> people working hard for the wrong motives.

Rather than arguing for their own *material* interests, they
were concerned about the individualising effects of working competitively for piece rates. Unity and commitment
were, for these women, the essential pre-conditions of the
co-operative's survival.

Olive and her friends, whose levels of skill were on the
whole the highest in the co-operative, had always ad-
vocated maintaining the distinction between skilled and
unskilled labour. They particularly resented the full-time
bench-workers being paid more than themselves. Furthermore, they often claimed that the difference in skill and
therefore productivity between individual women resulted
in an 'unfair' allocation of reward: 'Why should I make it up
for a slow machinist. I do as much in six hours as most of
them do in eight hours.' Members of this group might have
been prepared to raise the average intensity of their labour in
order to have even greater choice as to the times during
which it was exercised, and the piece-wage system could
easily have made this possible. However, Olive saw piece-
rates as being not only in her own, but also in the firm's
interest. Her commitment to Fakenham's continued existence was pragmatic and her previous work experience had
convinced her that people worked hardest under incentive
schemes:

> Nobody works hard without incentive schemes—faster and
> better workers have to be paid more. There's no other way
> of getting the work done.

Although she appreciated the relaxed atmosphere that
resulted from having no wage differentials,[3] she saw low
productivity as a major cause of the enterprise's failure and
therefore she pushed for incentives.

These opinions about incentives were expressed during
an interview at home with Olive at which her husband was
present. As a member of the National Graphical Associa-

tion, a traditional craft union which strongly supports wage differentials, he fully endorsed a differential pay scheme and talked about how well the bonus scheme worked at Cox and Wyman, where he was employed as a compositor:

> Two men do exactly the same job, but one takes home a few pounds more a day because he's a better worker. That's only fair. If you don't want to work hard, then you don't get the bonus.

A Mr K. of London: his profit, their loss

I arrived at the factory the following Monday to find K.'s machines installed. K. had arranged for Lilly, work-supervisor at his London factory, to spend a week in Fakenham training the ten machinists who were to work on the contract. The new atmosphere of optimism was striking. Most of the women were smartly dressed and looked more confident that I had ever seen them. Some, however, felt unable to share in this enthusiasm, being either worried or cynical about their prospects. Ironically enough, Nancy at this point was particularly cheerful, believing that this contract augured well for the future. She did not foresee the extent to which her own position would be undermined by these developments.

The contract was for producing skirts from pre-cut material and the labour process was subdivided into five discrete machining jobs, sewing up the side seams, setting the zip in, making up the waist bands; sewing the waist bands on; and hemming. Two machinists worked on each job. Lilly went about organising the work in her usual way. Her task was to train the machinists to complete each job in a specified time. This meant machining according to the results of a time study carried out in the London factory.[4]

There, work was organised in a production line and the workers were paid piece-work rates. At Fakenham, K. had set up his machines for a production line; this served to reduce face-to-face talk between the machinists, as well as taking control over the production process out of the women's hands. The ten machinists worked extremely hard, knowing that they had to prove their ability to produce the skirts in the specified time or the factory would lose the contract. Despite all their efforts, they were well behind the timings all week. Lilly regularly measuring their speed, pushed them on to work faster. Her job, too, was dependent on the productivity of the machinists. Whether as a result of this, or out of sympathy for the women, Lilly at first covered up their failure to meet the targets by helping out on the machines herself. But as a supervisor her room for manoeuvre was limited. She wanted to help them secure the contract, but also knew that K. would blame her if the skirts were produced too slowly.

Working on the K. contract served to polarise the women further. The Olive foursome were now even more physically isolated than they had been before, because of the way K's machines were arranged. Apart from the skirt contract, the only work in the factory was the tail-end of a shoe contract and this only involved bench-work. So they either did bench-work or were often left without any work to do. The ten machinists on the K. contract, by comparison, were working hard together and felt a renewed sense of solidarity. This was especially marked in the case of the five part-timers, who were now working full-time. They increasingly felt central to the fate of the co-operative and began to express stronger commitment to Fakenham Enterprises.

These five women all had school-age children. Three of the women asked me to collect their children from the local school and bring them back to the factory for an extra hour each day—so that they could work an eight-hour day. The children of the other two women were older and could be left at home for the extra hour on their own. The K. contract had acted as a catalyst on these women—forcing them to take a more active part in Fakenham's operations. During the following weeks, Nora was to take on increasing responsibility for organising the work. She had previously worked with Nancy at Sextons and now responded to Nancy's encouragement in the new situation. She began identifying with the founding members and gradually took on their attitudes with respect to the foursome:

> I'm prepared to work eight hours because I think that's what we've got to do to get the long-term contract and get back on our feet. There's a few people in this factory who aren't prepared to do anything for the factory. They're not pre- pared to do K.'s contract. And some people will tell you that they're shoe machinists. But I was a shoe machinist and I'm prepared to try my hand at something else. People have just got to be prepared to try their hand at anything.

Differences in the *kinds* of commitment to the co- operative became explicit a week after the contract had begun, when K. demanded twelve full-time machinists, instead of the agreed ten. It was more economical for him in the short term and it was also part of his strategy to make the enterprise totally dependent on his work. From the point of view of the factory, K. was making unreasonable demands. The women did not challenge this because they did not feel in a position to re-negotiate the terms of a deal Nancy had already agreed to. Furthermore, they were powerless— desperate for work. Outlining the firm's chronic financial problems, Nancy asked a meeting for extra volunteers to work full-time. The discussion that ensued took the form of a debate over whether the part-time workers should make 'sacrifices' in order to work full-time. Brenda accused Olive and her friends of not being prepared to go out of their way for the firm. Nancy announced that children would not be allowed into the factory during the school holidays. No reasons were given for this change of practice, but, although they were angry about it, the women accepted it. One of the part-time women suggested that there be two production lines on K.'s work—one full-time and one part- time—but this suggestion was ignored. Another woman suggested that women with school-age children be allowed to machine in their homes during the summer holidays.

Various people made comments about 'putting their children first'.

The meeting was upsetting for everyone and afterwards several women were arguing and crying. The part-timers felt torn between their need for a part-time job and the likelihood that the enterprise would fold if they refused to work full-time. Many of them blamed Nancy for putting them in such a dilemma and for pressuring them to work full-time. Seeing how hard the full-timers were working for no extra financial reward hardened the resolve of Olive's section *not* to work full-time. Olive was adamant that she would not work so hard on the production line for the same wage. K. had offered to pay piece-rates *direct* to the machinists, rather than paying a fixed amount to the firm. The production line he had set up would have made this easier to administer. Agreement to it, however, would have signalled the end of the women's control over Fakenham Enterprises' finances and a fundamental breakdown in the co-operative itself. Nancy, in agreement with the other founder members, continued to insist that K. pay a flat rate for the skirts to the enterprise. Olive and her friends resented this, even though piece-rate payment was not the accepted practice at the co-operative. They complained about not being consulted over the decision to refuse K.'s offer to pay by piece-rates or an individual bonus scheme.

The founding members, however, did not consider that Olive's section should have the same say in decision-making. During the weeks of the K. contract, they had been working long hours and Pat and Brenda, in particular, had machined until after 5 p.m. every night in the hope of making up enough skirts to satisfy K. They became increasingly hostile to Olive and her group and criticised the formal structure of the co-operative as a result. As Brenda said, referring to that group:

> Most of them leave at 3.30 p.m. sharp and won't work late when it's needed. But when it comes to decisions being made, they want to know everything and have a say in everything. It's not fair. I argue a lot with Nancy, mainly

about that. At the moment, everyone gets a share in the factory after working here six months, but not everyone pulls their weight. It shouldn't be like that. . . . Only the original women who sat-in should have shares. People who are only here for a job don't deserve a vote on decisions because they don't care about the factory.

The original women were working harder than ever before and in full view was Olive's foursome, sitting idle most of the day and yet being paid the same wage. It seemed to them as though they were 'sweating' directly for these four. As it was, they were subsidising the slow machinists on the production line, but they did not mind that because they saw themselves as working for the good of the firm. But never before had they been working so hard while Olive's section did nothing. Observing this, Brenda groaned:

How can you have a co-operative factory with those lot here who just treat this as a normal job. At 3.30 p.m. they're off and out regardless of what's needed.

In fact, the nature of the deal with K. *had* made it more like a 'normal job'.

It was because of their disillusionment with co-operative practice at Fakenham that Pat and Brenda changed their minds on the question of piece-rates. They now, for the first time, agreed with Olive in proposing this form of payment, but not for the same reasons. They now admitted that many women would leave the factory if there were good jobs available elsewhere. They also recognised that most women with school-age children would not work full-time. However, the main conclusion they drew from their experience was that most people would not work well in a co-operative system. Lack of unity and the formation of cliques made it impossible to run a co-operative properly, they said: 'You can't make decisions in that factory because everyone's against each other.'

The Beginning of the End

Having given K. control of the production process, the factory's remaining claim to co-operative status was its financial self-management. With agreement growing even among the founding members that K.'s proposed system of payment direct to the machinists should be accepted, the end of Fakenham Enterprises as a co-operative was inevitable. Sensing this, Nancy realised too late that her own position as organiser had also been eroded by the K. contract. While Lilly was in the factory, Nancy had stayed away for several days. Lilly organised and supervised the skirt machining, while Pat answered the telephone and dealt with any other business. When Nancy returned, she tried to assert her authority by reorganising some of the work. She was disturbed by the changed appearance of the factory:

> Fakenham Enterprises seems like an ordinary factory with people with their noses down. People aren't going to be willing to sit around and have discussions about things.

She was very upset and did not return to the factory for several more days. Cindy voiced her suspicions about the underlying cause of Nancy's anxiety: 'It's because Lilly is organising the production line and she doesn't like it when she isn't organising things.'

K. had planned to leave Lilly at the co-operative for only a week. At the beginning of the second week, he came to see whether his work would be done properly if she left. He arrived to find Nancy away and Pat in charge, on Nancy's authority. K. therefore approached Pat and Brenda to discuss who would supervise the production line after Lilly left. They went into the office with Edna and Natalia to discuss it further. If Nancy had been present, she would have been expected as usual to negotiate with K. In her absence, however, the women left on the production line started complaining about this informal clique taking over. 'This is a co-operative . . . we should all hear . . . who do they think they are, going into the office,' said Nora and the others murmured in agreement. These five women now felt, by virtue of their new full-time status, that their complaints about the founding members' special position were legitimate.

All the non-machinists, not only Nancy, were worried about the K. contract. Because K.'s contract only required machinists, they feared their own redundancy. Nancy, Edna and Natalia expressed this in terms of their anxiety that the co-operative would be transformed into an ordinary factory and, ultimately, taken over by K. They tried to take on other small contracts, both to provide them with some bench-work and to retain some independence of K. However, these contracts came into the factory less and less often. As a result of this lack of work, several of the bench-workers left the factory. These women had never felt involved in the co-operative and, being unskilled, had no particular commitment to the job. By now it was increasingly the case that only machinists had a role to play in the factory. Although Nancy was still nominally in charge, the work was not adequately supervised. There was organisational confusion in which can be seen the first step towards the collapse of the enterprise. Meetings became less frequent and the women were openly cynical about the factory's prospects. Fakenham Enterprises was soon to lose all the characteristics of a co-operative and would resemble a group of outworkers, gathered together under one roof.

An Unhappy Ending

In the summer of 1975, when the fieldwork for this research was being carried out, Fakenham Enterprises was on the verge of collapse but still looking for contracts. Although they had managed to defend their autonomy, the women's morale had been irreversibly weakened. Arguments between them about the possibility of payment by piece-rates had come to a head, and the case against such a system was losing ground. As it transpired, K. cancelled his contract but the threat to the co-operative's independence did not disappear with it.

When the K. contract was withdrawn, the only offer of work came from a Mr. E. who, as owner of a Thetford clothing firm, had advertised in Fakenham for outworkers to machine dresses. Whereas K. was based in London and wanted only full-time machinists, E. operated from much nearer Fakenham and was prepared to take on part-time workers. As a result of negotiations between him and Nancy a contract was signed on 2 October.[5] Although there was initially some expectation that Mr. E. would be concerned with the development of Fakenham Enterprises as a co-operative, as the main supplier of work he quickly assumed a position of authority and control.

E., like K. before him, required machinists only; he installed twelve machines in the factory and supplied all the materials. Most of the women were put to work on this contract, trained and supervised by E. Those who were not machinists, including several of the founding members, found themselves without a role at the factory. Towards Christmas 1975, with the firm totally dependent on the E. contract, these women were laid off. The machinists, who stayed on, were glad of the comparatively regular work and payment. By this time the guaranteed minimum rate had been abolished and a piece-work system was operating. As E. took more explicit control of the enterprise, tensions mounted between Nancy and the rest of the workforce. E. started paying the machinists directly and by March 1976 had stopped paying Nancy at all. Fakenham Enterprises as a financially self-managed factory no longer existed.

When I visited the factory in the summer of 1977, all that remained was a group of machinists working for E., none of whom had been involved in the establishment of the co-operative. It had become an outpost of Thetford Clothing.

7 Wives, Mothers, Workers

The lives of the Fakenham women, in the factory and in the home, were formed by the facts that they were *working class,* and that they were *women*. Having examined the workplace I now move outside it, to look at the domestic sphere. I will concentrate on the significance of the fact that the Fakenham workers were women.

In Chapter 1 I looked at how women's entry into, and experience of, wage labour differs from men's. This difference both follows from and reinforces women's and men's distinct relations with the family. But much of the literature on women workers discussed in Chapter 1 has little to say about working–class women. These authors deal with the problems of married women workers primarily in middle-class terms. The Fakenham workers, however, are *not* women for whom the 'choice' to work is new and attractive. Rather, they are the women of the working class, who have traditionally always had to work. Like that of their mothers before them, their desire for a job is shaped by economic necessity. Their occupational history is of jobs at the lower end of the labour market—largely part-time or casual, unskilled work.[1] And given their husbands' similarly low pay, these women's wages are an essential part of the household income, especially at certain stages in the domestic life-cycle.

I have already pointed out the tendency to ignore the very different situations of women at different points in the family life-cycle. Even the best of the studies discussed in Chapter 1 for the most part only distinguishes between single women and married women with children. As a result, important distinctions *within* the category of married women are obscured. Further, insofar as women's position in the life-cycle is explored it is largely in terms of childcare constraints. But childcare is only part of the story. There is both more and less to family life than mother's love: domestic drudgery and money calculations, for example. While this has been recognised in previous research, there has been a failure to integrate all the diverse aspects of women's domestic and work lives as they vary with the life-cycle. This narrative has revealed substantial differences in 'commitment' among the Fakenham women— both to work in general and to working at the Fakenham co-operative. These differences demonstrate the significance of drawing further distinctions in the life-cycle; it is to this that we now turn.

In and Out of the Labour Market: the impact of the life-cycle

If we adopt Beynon and Blackburn's distinctions between five stages in the life-cycle, it is the fourth stage in which the family budget is under the most strain and, consequently, the time at which the wife's income is most needed.[2] This period, when the financial pressures on family finances are greatest, begins when the youngest child enters school and ends when the children become financially independent. The reason that this stage does not start earlier, when the children are at pre-school age, is not a lack of financial incentives for women to work. Rather, wives do not generally enter employment during this period because of their responsibility for children, and this is largely true *whatever* the financial strain involved. Women are responsible for childcare not *a priori*, but because of social conventions — it is expected by their husbands and accepted by the women themselves.

Being married women with school-age children, the part-time workers at Fakenham Enterprises were at this fourth stage of the life-cycle.[3] They worked in order to contribute to the family income, but clearly gave priority to their family roles. The co-operative provided them with convenient hours, enabling them to take time off during school holidays and when their children were sick. The less skilled machinists' experience of the labour market was of monotonous, temporary jobs. They therefore had the lowest expectations of the intrinsic job-content, although their expectations were raised when Fakenham gave them the opportunity to escape from unskilled work by becoming machinists. However, the part-time status of these workers was one reason why they were less involved in the actual organisation of the co-operative. Olive, Blonde Sue, Ann and Molly were also less involved than the full-timers, though not for the same reasons. For such skilled machinists, Fakenham had a dual appeal. It not only provided convenient hours, but also a relatively satisfying job in which they could exercise their skills. They appreciated that the factory was co-operatively organised, but felt excluded and regretted that their hours of childcare inhibited their fuller involvement in the co-operative.

In sum, the part-time workers of both groups had to work because of their need for the money — but the practicalities of childcare meant that they could only work part-time. During my stay at the factory the part-timers felt torn between their need for part-time jobs and the likelihood that the enterprise would collapse if they refused to work full-time. They were caught in this dilemma by the advent of the K. contract. In response, some of the part-timers started working longer hours, taking on more responsibility, and identifying with the co-operative—even though they had school-age children. Their two needs, to work at Fakenham and to work part-time, were initially compatible. They became contradictory when the K. contract, requiring full-time shifts, was introduced. Inevitably, these women's potential for fuller involvement in the co-operative was circumscribed by the combined constraints of childcare and financial strain.

In Chapter 5, we saw that the women who were able to play an active and central role in the co-operative were (with one exception) women without heavy domestic duties. Free from childcare, they were also relatively free of financial pressures. They were single or, if married, either without children or with children who were economically independent. They needed to work, but could survive periods of low pay with less hardship than the other women.

These full-time workers had a different *kind* of commitment, both to working in general and to working at Fakenham Enterprises. To them, the work itself, as distinct from the income and convenient hours, was an important part of their lives. As a co-operative venture, Fakenham was a special work situation, and this would suggest the need for a greater commitment to the enterprise. As a result of their experience of the occupation, they had responded to this demand; identifying with Fakenham Enterprises as 'their' factory, their commitment to it was related to it being run as a co-operative. Complaining that the part-timers only worked for the money, they tended to regard the genuine constraints of childcare merely as consequences of the part-timers' attitudes. However, their participation, both in the original occupation and in the co-operative, was conditional on their stage in the life-cycle—that is, freedom from childcare. Thus, although women are usually regarded as having a lower commitment to work than men, it was possible for these women to be considerably more involved in their enterprise than most men are in their (non–co–operative) workplaces.

There were, however, four other women on the full–time shift who did not share this high commitment to the co–operative: Jenny and Val, Grace and Phoebe. Two of these were young, single women who were just learning to machine and the other two were older, married women doing unskilled work, one of whom was childless, while the other had children who no longer lived at home. The single women saw their job as a temporary phase before marriage, while the older women were working to escape the loneli–ness of home. The absence of financial pressures on these four women was reflected in their low commitment to Fakenham Enterprises as an employer. And, because they had not been involved in the original occupation, they were similarly uncommitted to Fakenham Enterprises as a co–operative.

So their life–cycle positions had a major impact on the Fakenham women's commitment to work in general and to the co–operative. This cannot be reduced to childcare con–straints alone. We need to look at the way in which the domestic economy as a whole is organised. Childcare can then be seen as one part of what is generally understood to be women's work within the family. According to this sexual division of labour, the Fakenham women were expected to sustain the household economy, both by engaging in paid work and by performing housework.

Domestic Division of Labour

'I don't keep a dog and bark myself'

In the first chapter it was argued that women's experience of wage labour must be analysed with reference to both the organisation of the household economy and the division of labour within it. Studies of housework have tended to define 'housework' as something engaged in by women only, excluding men from their scope. But the housework performed by women must be seen in relation to their husbands' domestic work. This section will examine the distribution of housework or, more comprehensively, the domestic division of labour within the families of the Fakenham women; the aim is to understand how participation in the co-operative was contingent upon the domestic work-load borne by the women.

What emerges from my data does not correspond with Young and Willmott's (1975) picture of symmetry outlined earlier. According to this picture the entry of married women into paid employment gives rise to the symmetrical family. The data presented here suggest that women as housewives still retain primary responsibility for, and do, most of the housework, including childcare. When I was asking the Fakenham women and their husbands about housework their answers revealed a marked uniformity in the sexual division of labour within their households. On the whole, the men always did the 'outdoor' jobs— mowing the lawn, gardening, fixing the car, household repairs and, to a lesser extent, painting and decorating. Table 5 is based on wives' responses. The husbands' responses were essentially the same, except in relation to washing-up, where they were less ready to acknowledge that they helped. Only three husbands mentioned doing so. The one exception to this general pattern was Edna's husband, the postman, who worked shifts and was therefore at home most afternoons. He was the only husband who genuinely shared his wife's housework—shopping, cooking and washing-up. At the other extreme, two husbands did nothing at all in this area: 'I don't keep a dog and bark myself' was the way one of them put it.

While the husbands did have a responsibility for performing certain household tasks, these had very different characteristics from those the women performed. Most strikingly, they might be seen as neither routine nor continuous, being a few substantial tasks performed at intervals, frequently outdoors. By comparison, the dominant characteristic of women's housework is precisely that it is 'never done'. Cooking, washing and cleaning are a con-

Table 5 Domestic division of labour. This Table is based on wives' answers to the following questions:

Are there certain household jobs that you always do?   Are there jobs that your husband always does?

Who decides what major things to buy for the house?   (N = 19 in most cases. For activities related to children, N = 11.)

Activity	Who does it					
	wife always	usually wife	do together	either	usually husband	husband always
Buying major items	1		15	1		1
Making and mending clothes	19					
Ironing	19					
Cleaning house	16	2				
Cooking	16	1		1	1	
Shopping: general	14	1	3	1		
Washing-up	12	3	3	1		
Window-cleaning	12	2	2	1		2
Feeding children	10	1				
Putting children to bed	7	1		2		1
Decorating	5	1	4	1	1	6
Digging the garden	2		4	1	1	9
Repairing the car				1		13
Mowing the lawn	1			1		16
Household repairs	1					18

tinuous process of maintenance and service. Of course, this contrast is exaggerated and depends partly on conventional conceptions; lawn-mowing, for instance, is just as continuous as window-cleaning. Nevertheless, there is a general distinction which is reinforced by popular evaluations. Indeed, these evaluations are intrinsic to the domestic division of labour. For example, it is in a chapter on *leisure* that Young and Willmott (1975) discuss these 'male' activities in the home. At no point do they reflect on how these jobs, rather than women's domestic tasks, come to be seen as 'leisure' activities. However, there is an implicit assumption that the relationship of men and women to paid employment is different and that this difference structures the domestic division of labour. Men's work is paid work and their work in the home is a form of 'non-work'; women, in contrast, work in the home.

The domestic division of labour between the sexes is unequal in a double sense; a far greater share of the tasks falls to the wife, and these tasks are also regarded as less skilled. As in the labour market, the definition of skill here has more to do with the value attributed to men's activities as against women's, than with the intrinsic nature of the jobs. With tasks so clearly demarcated according to gender, domestic work is unlikely to be a central area for disputes between wives and husbands. It is taken for granted that housewives perform these endlessly repetitious household chores.

The Fakenham women's domestic burden was not significantly affected by their involvement in the co-operative. When asked whether their husbands had assumed additional household responsibilities during this time, ten women said no. The other eight replied in the affirmative, but said simply that their husbands occasionally helped with the washing up. When interviewed independently, all the husbands confirmed what their wives had said. To get a more detailed account of their domestic activities, I asked all the women and their husbands to keep a daily diary. As a day in the life of Olive exemplifies, the Fakenham women did two jobs while working at the enterprise— all their housework as well as their wage work. This necessarily limited the extent of their participation in the co-operative.

Olive's diary of domestic tasks on a typical weekday:

Before work   Packs lunch for herself and her husband
                     Feeds daughter breakfast
                     Washes dishes
                     Makes beds
                     Makes a cup of tea
                     Takes daughter to school

After work   Picks daughter up from school
                     Cooks supper
                     Washes up
                     Vacuum cleans

Recreation   Knits and watches T.V.

Olive's husband's tasks on a typical weekday:

Before work   Drinks tea

After work   Walks dog
                     Gardens or watches T.V.

Olive's diary on a Sunday:

Morning   Prepares breakfast
                     Cooks lunch
                     Makes beds
                     Irons
                     Vacuum cleans and dusts

Afternoon   Washes up
                     Goes for a drive or does some gardening

Evening   Cooks
                     Washes up
                     Baths daughter
                     Sews and mends or watches T.V.

Olive's husband on a Sunday:

Morning   Works on the car
                  Mows the lawn or gardens

Afternoon   As above, or goes for a drive with Olive

Evening   Watches T.V.

Olive was in the fourth stage of the life-cycle. Below is Natalia's diary; she was an older woman whose children had already left home. Although Olive and Natalia were in different stages of the life-cycle, their diaries look very similar.

Natalia's diary of domestic tasks on a typical weekday:

Before work   Cooks breakfast
                  Washes dishes
                  Makes beds

After work   Cooks tea
                  Washes up
                  Irons
                  Cleans

Recreation   Watches T.V.

Natalia's husband's tasks on a typical weekday:

Before work   Nothing

After work   Gardens
                  Watches T.V.

Natalia's diary on a Sunday:

Morning   Prepares breakfast
                  Cooks dinner
                  Bakes
                  Washes up
                  Cleans and tidies

Afternoon	Goes for a drive
Evening	Prepares meal
	Washes up
	Watches T.V.

Natalia's husband on a Sunday:

Morning	Fixes car, or
	Does Repairs outside the house
Afternoon	Goes for a drive
Evening	Watches T.V.

Although all housewives do roughly the same housework, it does fluctuate with the life-cycle. A comparison of the diaries indicates, as one might expect, that the amount of housework a woman does is reduced when her children leave home. Even so, for the women most actively involved in the co-operative, the sexual division of labour was not altered. Far from supporting the Young and Willmott thesis that increasing symmetry results from married women working, these data suggest that the amount and type of housework done by the Fakenham women was hardly modified by their engagement in paid work.

The notion of symmetry refers not only to the sharing of housework; it also encompasses the sharing of decision-making. Table 5 shows that the only task which the vast majority of Fakenham wives and husbands did together was 'buying major items'. Superficially, this might suggest increased symmetry. However, as we shall see presently, in the context of social relations between wives and husbands, a more convincing explanation may be that husbands retain control over major decisions, and hence the purchase of major items.[4]

In conclusion, while not all housework is done by women, neither is it shared. The family is still asymmetrical—a clear division of labour exists, according to which the wife does the jobs which add systematically to the day's work. The fact that these women were working outside the home too did not prevent them from carrying a dispropor- tionately heavy domestic burden. Nor had their partici- pation in the struggles of the co-operative resulted in any perceptible increase in the amount of housework under- taken by most husbands. Although it was important to the women themselves, the independence gained through their experience of work found no expression within the family. This differential distribution of tasks between wives and husbands intersects with a similarly unequal allocation of resources, which we will now go on to discuss.

Household Economy

The paucity of empirical studies on the structure of the domestic economy has already been mentioned. The con- cept of the household, with its concomitant image of all family members having equal call on a collective income, remains in current use. It has major repercussions both on social policy· formation and on pay bargaining, where the notion of the 'family wage' still dominates.[5] This is despite (or because of) the fact that little is known about the distri- bution of the family income *between* its members—a prob- lem mentioned by Michael Young in 1952 which persists.[6] The management and distribution of resources *within* the household is still an unexplored area. From such work as has been done, it emerges that the differential distribution of tasks between wives and husbands is mirrored by a similarly unequal allocation of resources. But the assumption remains that the family can be treated as a unity of interests, with consumption simply measured in terms of equal dis- tribution within households. There is a sense in which the family is indeed a unity of interests; the notion of 'family' implies that all members are concerned with the welfare of the unit as a whole. What is ignored is that the organisation of the domestic economy creates the basis for conflicts of interest between wives and husbands over money. The argument here, then, is that marriage is a site of structured inequality, in which wives are relegated to a position of economic dependence.

The 'housewife's calculation', based on the structure of individual domestic economies, involves a different conception of the household economy from that held by men. This is because women manage the household budget, as well as performing housework.[7] The husband usually takes money for his private consumption *before* the domestic budget is calculated and spent, while the wife's individual share is not a separate allocation at all.[8] Rather, it is the part of the household budget that is left over *after* family needs have been met.

Such consideration as has been given to the existence of conflicting interests within the family tends to treat women's apparent control over household consumption patterns as evidence of their power in the family. For example, in attempting to measure differences of 'power' between husbands and wives, Blood and Wolfe (1960) treat control over decisions as to what to buy as a central indicator of power within marriage.[9] The position of women, and the relationship between wives and husbands in the domestic economy, however, varies substantially according to their general class circumstances. In working-class homes, women's 'power' over consumption patterns is extremely limited. Wives do the shopping, but because of a tight budget, the element of choice about what to buy is severely restricted. Consumption patterns fundamentally depend on the size of the family income. Further, despite the lack of supporting evidence, it is at least plausible to argue that the person with the 'power' over, or responsibility for, household budgeting is the person most likely to do without when earnings fall short. This could be interpreted as an effect of the ideology of maternity, which encourages self-sacrifice. Women as wives and mothers usually consume the least for themselves, as they subsume their own needs under family needs.[10] Finally, all these discussions miss the fact that women's decisions about how to use the 'housekeeping' money, are taken only after the decision about the proportion of the net family income allocated to them for 'housekeeping'.

I have stressed throughout that the Fakenham women's earnings were essential to their households. Many of these families would have come near the 'poverty line' without the wife's income. If the yardstick of low pay as £40 per week, used in Chapter 3, is again used as a reference point, it can be seen from Table 4 that nearly half of the Fakenham families in this study would have fallen below such a poverty line. Of the nineteen husbands, only eight earned more than £40 per week and only a few of these significantly more. In most cases, the women's wages were necessary to keep the family's living standards above poverty level, or to keep them from approaching it.[11] As we have seen, however, the severity of the financial strain on the family depends on its position in the life-cycle—the fourth stage being the worst. The fact that these women go out to work may mean that an increased proportion of the net family income is under their control. Even so, we will see that the Fakenham women did not spend a large proportion of their wages on themselves.

There were roughly two alternative structures for the organisation of the household economy. In neither case was income pooled. There were, instead, separate allocations of money whereby the husband's and wife's wages were spent differently. In both cases, the husband paid the big bills. Pat's remarks were fairly representative: 'We keep our money separate. I do the housekeeping on mine, and my husband pays the big bills.' Either the women's wage was directly spent on 'housekeeping' (basically food), or the husband gave the wife a 'housekeeping' allowance— typically ranging from £15–£17 a week, and even as little as £10 in one case. In this case, the wife's money was spent on clothes and consumer durables and, to a varying degree, topped up an inadequate housekeeping allowance. Overall, husbands either received pocket-money or, more commonly, seemed to keep the indeterminate amounts left over after they had paid the big bills.

As we have seen, the pay at Fakenham Enterprises was

generally low and there were often wage cuts. The effect of this was that the women typically cut down on 'family' expenditure by making personal sacrifices— doing without a haircut or clothes or make-up for themselves. There was no evidence to suggest that their husbands accepted a corresponding cut in their own pocket-money. Unlike the men, the women felt that their own individual needs were somehow 'extras' and the most easily expendable items. It was only when they had to sacrifice what they considered to be essential family needs that they seriously thought about leaving the factory. In the short term, they were willing to work for low wages and cut down on family needs so that the factory could survive; to ensure the continuity of their employment. But even the most committed women could not sustain this for long.

Brenda was the only member of the founding group who was in the fourth stage of the life cycle— that is, the stage when financial strain is greatest. She was exceptionally committed to the co-operative, being the only full-time worker with school-age children. The long hours she worked at the factory had been a source of mounting tension with her husband, as well as resulting in considerable physical and mental strain on herself. For over three years she had withstood these pressures, but then the financial strain became unbearable:

> It was all right three years ago—the pound went further then— you could manage. But, now, with the inflation, you can't afford to be without a wage for a few weeks.

She left Fakenham Enterprises soon afterwards, complaining that she could not even afford to buy shoes for her sons.

None of the women reported any *variations* in the amount of money they received— there was no suggestion that if the husband earned more, a wife received more as a result.[12] More significantly, no-one mentioned that her husband increased his contribution to the housekeeping as compensation for the decline in earnings at Fakenham Enterprises.

Most husbands were hostile to the enterprise because of the low pay. As one husband typically remarked:

> That place has never been any good—they are working just to keep the place barely going. I can't see no future in it. She doesn't get proper wages. It's the uncertainty of the wages.

Some women even feared facing their husbands on a pay-day when there had been wage-cuts. The husbands' complaints were frequent, despite the absence of alternative employment, particularly for the part-time workers. The husbands' complaint, then, was not 'Why don't you go elsewhere?' but was based on expectations of higher earnings. The husbands assessed Fakenham Enterprises as an ordinary employer and therefore expected the women to earn more. The size of the wage packet was their sole consideration.

However, it was the women themselves, rather than their husbands and children, who suffered from the firm's low pay. Earning money did not alter the Fakenham women's traditional position in the family. Although they were earning, it was they, and not their husbands, who made the sacrifices when money fell short. The financial strain and its meaning for women is thus dependent on the organisation of the domestic economy. To understand the wider significance of the fact that it is *women* who manage the household budget, we shall now go on to discuss the ideology of domesticity.

The Ideology of Domesticity

> the man in the domestic household is held to be the breadwinner, the worker, whilst the wife works for 'the extras'. Very often, of course, the material importance of her wage may be much greater than this suggests, and certainly her domestic labour is the lynchpin of the whole household economy. The wage packet as a kind of symbol

of machismo dictates the domestic culture and economy
and tyrannises both men and women

(*Willis, 1977:150*).

The special situation of the founding women, who were
relatively free to work without pay, cannot be generalised
to a statement about all women workers, or even to all those
at Fakenham Enterprises. The economic constraints were
very different for the full-time and part-time groups; and
yet, what is striking is the similarity of the *attitudes* in both
groups to the income generated by their work. The
ideology of domesticity means that married women's
wages, even if essential, have the appearance of being
secondary. To both groups, the husband's wage packet was
seen as providing subsistence, whereas the wife's was seen
as supplementary. This was true even of the part-time
workers, who were most in need of the money.

The ideology of the male breadwinner is reinforced by
the common allocation of money whereby the husband's
and wife's wage is spent on different things. Such items as
rent and fuel bills, which men pay, are considered to be the
necessities of life. By contrast, women's responsibility for
the day-to-day spending mirrors the petty, repetitious,
never-ending nature of housework. So women's purchase
of food for the family is somehow defined as routine rather
than necessary. As we have seen with regard to housework,
the popular representation of household income as shared
between husbands and wives has had some exposure in
Fakenham. Quite a few women said that their family's
income was pooled and then went on to tell me about who
paid for what. For example, Phoebe: 'We [my husband and
I] pool all our income, but I spend mine on housekeeping.
He keeps some money and pays the mortgage and the big
bills.'

The women with families to support did not, unlike their
husbands, expect to spend any of the money they earned on
themselves. Here I would argue that a significant dis-
junction exists between the Fakenham women's *stated*

motives for working and how they actually *spent* their wages, which indicates something about why, in fact, they went out to work. Nearly all the women said that they wanted to work and gave their reasons as a combination of wanting company and wanting to 'feel a bit independent' of their husbands. This sense of independence seemed to derive as much from simply being in paid employment as from the money itself. Nevertheless, it is clear that their desire for a job was primarily determined by economic necessity and the absence of any real alternative. That is, the only available alternative to having a job was to be isolated at home in rather harsh financial circumstances. Work patterns for these women, as they corresponded to the various stages of the life-cycle, were taken for granted, so that to mention money as the main reason for working seemed somewhat irrelevant—as it would be to ask men why they work. Given that they had to work, companion-ship became the prime reward at work.

The Domestic Identity

What *meaning* did working outside the home have for the Fakenham women? The context for understanding the atti-tudes expressed by the Fakenham women themselves is provided by a consideration of women's psychological identification with the domestic world. For both women and men, the experience of work is mediated by their posi-tion in the family. This chapter has argued that working-class women and men occupy sexually differentiated spheres and that this leads to diverging perceptions of work. Whereas men's identity and work roles are relatively inte-grated, for women work as a source of social identity is largely displaced by the domestic roles of wife and mother, as defined by social class and culture.

Fundamentally, it was as wives and mothers that the women at Fakenham Enterprises viewed their fellow workers. Even the women most centrally involved in the co-operative did not question this. Although they rarely saw each other outside their work lives, as Fakenham is a small town they did know about each other's domestic situations. They brought this knowledge into the work-place and considered it directly relevant to their shopfloor discussions. For example, when the number of full-time workers had to be increased, Molly's refusal to transfer from the part-time to the full-time shift was censured because everyone knew that she was childless. Cindy, on the other hand, would have liked to have worked longer hours and become more involved in the organisation of the co-operative, but felt unable to do so because of her family duties:

> I'm not prepared to take on responsibility because I consider the job temporary. I have to move whenever my husband moves. Women have too many other commitments to their family to take on a lot of responsibility at work.

Sharing this outlook, the other women did not expect her to work full-time.

All the women were adamant that mothers with pre-school children should stay at home to look after them. Only Jackie, a part-time worker, regularly brought her four-year-old child into the factory with her—this was necessitated by her husband's extremely irregular employ-ment. Even so, Jackie's practice was often criticised by her fellow workers.[13] Once, when Jackie arrived at the factory with her child quite ill, she was greeted with such strong disapproval that she immediately took the child home. Edna summed up the prevalent sentiments of the women towards working mothers, as follows:

> Ideally all mothers would stay at home for the first five years after having children. You shouldn't expect the best of both worlds—work and kids. . . . No, nurseries wouldn't be the answer. Why should someone else take over the responsi-bility of looking after your kids? They grow away from you so fast anyway—you want to have them with you all the time until they're at least five so that you can mould them.

The belief that a woman's primary duty is to her family was so ingrained that none of the women questioned the assumption that Jackie's family responsibilities were more important than any loss of production that her absence from the factory might cause. Such an assumption would clearly not operate in relation to men's work. For all the mothers working at the enterprise, the most common reason given for not coming to work was a child's illness. It was they, and not their husbands, who had to adjust their working lives around childcare.

The Fakenham women fully identified with motherhood, not wanting to go out to work when they had young children. Although, practically speaking, there were no alternative childcare facilities in Fakenham, these women did not see this as an explanation of their attitudes. Few of the women said they would use nurseries, even if they were provided at a price they could afford. (Clearly, it was difficult for them to imagine the possibility of good nurseries being available in Fakenham.) They valued the rewards associated with motherhood, seeing this as one of the most fulfilling periods of a woman's life. Nevertheless, this commitment to motherhood created problems in their wish to work, as shown by the following incident related by one of the women:

> That's how I lost my last job. . . . In the school holidays I took my daughter to the neighbour's to look after her. She refused to stay there and said that I shouldn't be going to work and leaving her. She was very upset and crying. And I had a good cry and phoned my employer and said that I couldn't come.

At another level, any failure to fulfil the duties of motherhood resulted in considerable guilt. The guilt experienced by this woman resulted as much from an accurate assessment of the poor quality of the childcare she had resorted to as from an identification with being a mother. The effect of this, together with the nature of the employment open to these women, helps to explain this overwhelming preference for the mother role.

When discussing their reasons for engaging in paid employment, few of the Fakenham women referred to the money itself and it was almost never their initial response. Instead, they stressed the value of companionship at work compared with the boredom and isolation of being at home. All the women shared Cindy's reasons for 'enjoying' work:

> When you're home all day on your own there's no stimulus. There's nothing. I see nobody except my children. When you're home, you miss the company and the constant activity.

The common pattern for these women was to establish close and loyal friendships at work. These relationships, as for most working women, were based entirely in the workplace and had no expression outside it. This meant that the married women, particularly, relied on the membership of the work group remaining stable; they found it distressing if a friend had to leave the job. One woman gave the following account of how she experienced this:

> I used to have a great friend here who worked on the machine next to mine. We got on extremely well and always laughed together, as well as getting our work done. She's left the area and I miss her a lot. It made all the difference having her here at Fakenham.

Why is it that women rate company as an important reason for working and men usually do not?[14] It is so much part of a man's self-definition that he engages in paid work to support his family that no further explanation is expected. On the other hand, it is generally assumed to be characteristic of women that they work for adult company. This is partly a result of the women's role in the family not being considered that of a breadwinner. The social isolation of housewives, as compared to men, also leads them to prize companionship at work more highly. This is not to imply that men do not value the social rewards of work, but that the nature of their economic and domestic responsibilities gives such rewards a different significance. The unquestioned assumptions about married women's motives for working are thus reinforced by their expressed appreciation of companionship. All the Fakenham women who were mothers had stayed at home to look after their children until they were old enough to go to school. Despite their desire to do this, it had nevertheless been a period of severe isolation for them. This was not true for their husbands, who had more opportunities to go out. The men in Fakenham met each other in the evenings more frequently than did the women; sometimes on allotments during the summer, or in the pubs and work clubs in the area. Leaving their wives at home, over half of them went out at least once a week—usually to the pub or to play sport. The women, on the other hand, rarely, if ever, went out without husbands. The few who did either went to church or had a regular date with their mothers at the pub or bingo hall. As we saw in the earlier discussion of housework, most spent their evenings on household chores and seldom had any free time before going to bed at night.

The factor that was mentioned most often—after the companionship—was the feeling of independence they got from earning a wage, linked with the opportunity to spend money on 'extras'. Having mentioned the company, one of the part-timers went on to say:

> I like being independent of my husband. What I earn is mine—I don't have to take things out of the housekeeping money, for example, to buy a dress.

Many of the women expressed these sentiments. This would seem to indicate that economic need is no longer the main motive for married women's work outside their homes. Sociological studies, such as *Women's Two Roles,* would have us believe that 'psychological motives', such as a need for company and independence, are more important. Certainly at some stages of the life-cycle the woman's wage is more important that at others. But, as we have seen, all the Fakenham wives' wages were indeed necessary to the family income.

What was surprising was that even women in the fourth life-cycle stage, working part-time, saw their earnings as a source of independence although, in fact, this money was spent on their children and the house, and rarely on the wife's private consumption. These women's wages did *not* alter their basic position as economic dependants of their husbands. However, it did give them, independently of their husbands, increased spending power in their capacities as wives and mothers—a significant area of their lives. For these women, independence may just have meant being able to buy things for the children without having to ask their husbands for the money or for permission.[15] In this limited sense, working did result in some degree of autonomy for these women. They could thus live their dependent role with a greater sense of independence; this constitutes much of the significance of wage labour for married women. However, we should not let this obscure the fundamental, taken-for-granted importance of simply bringing in money.

From this discussion of married women's attitudes to paid employment, then, it emerges that the constraints limiting the impact of the distinctive experience of working in a co-operative were related to women's work situation in general. As with a conventional job, they experienced the conflict of identifying with the housewife–mother role while having to work for the money. On the whole, the nature of the jobs available to these women ruled out the possibility of intrinsic rewards, making company the principal compensation. The Fakenham women saw them-selves and were seen as housewives and mothers, a view reinforced by their husbands' attitudes towards their wages; men acknowledged the need for the wife's wage and yet saw it as supplementary.

The consequence of this ideology of domesticity, in conjunction with the social arrangements consistent with it, was such that even the experience of working at Fakenham Enterprises did not profoundly alter relations within the family. Rather, the impact of working in the co-operative mainly found expression in the work-sphere. At home, the distribution of resources and tasks grounded in sexual divisions was not affected by the women's involvement at the factory. Even for the original full-timers, who had gained most from this work experience, the self-confidence and new-found ability to assume organisational responsi-bility had little bearing on their home lives. In the end, like their previous jobs, the Fakenham co-operative was relegated to a subsidiary role in their lives. The wider question of how their political consciousness was shaped by this experience will be elaborated in the next and final chapter.

Eastern Counties Newspapers Ltd.

8   Experience and Consciousness

> I don't believe in politics. We just work and that's all
> (*Natalia*).

What was the relation between the Fakenham women's consciousness and their experience of working in a co-operative? In this chapter I shall discuss trade unionism and the role of trade unions in the occupation, and the elements which made up the women's political consciousness. I shall be arguing that it is important to distinguish between attitudes that pertain to people's lives, addressing their concrete experience, and general attitudes about society at large. Although *some* of the women could be said to have been radicalised at the factory level, the experience of working at the co-operative had little impact on their general political perspective. Thus, their work experience at Fakenham Enterprises did *not* alter their political consciousness at the societal level.

Life on a Co-operative Shopfloor

From the outset, it was clear that the women did not establish the co-operative at Fakenham with any explicitly political objectives in mind. The initial occupation, which launched the co-operative, was wholly contingent on the lack of alternative sources of employment. None of the women saw their act as a political gesture to begin with; the militancy that developed was a defensive response to the threat of redundancy. The experience of the occupation did, however, radicalise those who participated in it. These women identified with the co-operative and were to play a central role in it throughout its existence. They viewed the venture differently from the other women who joined later—many of whom spoke of it as 'just another job'. Thus, the co-operative did *not* have a uniform significance for all the women who worked there. At this juncture, therefore, I shall elaborate the differing conceptions of the co-operative held by the women.

Identification with the enterprise as their own was, as we have seen, primarily characteristic of the women originally involved, who spoke of it as 'our factory'. For Nancy, Fakenham Enterprises represented 'an ideal' of how people should work together. Fundamental to this ideal was shared decision-making; 'people aren't afraid to talk here . . . when we make a decision, it's an overall decision by everybody'. Nancy was convinced that:

> If we closed tomorrow we would have achieved something, because the people here have a greater measure of self-confidence now—they don't just want to be told what to do.

Other women endorsed this view, stating the best feature of working there as 'having a say in what goes on'; being able to 'talk a problem out'. They were quick to draw the analogy with a family business—on the one hand 'you've got freedom to take time off' and on the other 'you work bloody harder and you've got more worry'. Always a realist, Edna saw this freedom as existing only within limitations: 'you can't really expect to run a business and be able to do exactly as you like because you're cutting your own throat all the time'. She shared with the other founding members a pride in proving by example that a factory could be run co-operatively by its workers.

Having been involved in its formation, these women developed a self-conscious awareness of the political significance of Fakenham's co-operative status, which distinguished them from the rest of the women. While a few of the others did make reference to the fact that it was 'not like an ordinary factory—you're working for yourselves', only one woman, whose sister had taken part in the occupation, acknowledged the enterprise's wider signi-ficance. She alone emphasised her part-ownership of the factory, and saw it as a unique achievement for women to have taken control of the business. 'It's a real stroke for women,' she said, 'they're always looked down on at work. Women have to fight hard for everything they want.' For all the other women who joined after its formation, Fakenham Enterprises provided 'a job like any other'; its status as a co-operative had no particular meaning for them, and many were only dimly aware that they were indeed working in a co-operative. It has already been stressed that, as part-timers, these women considered that 'the best thing about Fakenham Enterprises is the convenient hours'. Their child-care responsibilities made them particularly appreciative of the opportunity to synchronise their working hours with school hours: 'what other factory lets you bring children with you during the school holidays?' In addition, they mentioned the relaxed atmosphere as one of the most positive aspects of their workplace:

There isn't a strained atmosphere here—you're left to get on with your work ... there's no supervisor looking over your shoulder the whole time.

Some went so far as to say: 'It's like a home from home.' Nevertheless, what predominated in their daily experience of working in the co-operative was the endless uncertainty of wages and work:

It seems so unstable. Some days there's a lot of work and some days there's none ... it's so disorganised that you don't know whether you're coming or going.

This insecurity was felt even more keenly by the founding members, who considered themselves directly responsible for the firm's survival. As well as worrying about their own pay packets, they were also concerned about the survival of the co-operative itself. Fakenham Enterprises' failure to become economically viable was, to them, a continuing source of frustration and confusion: 'We seem to be hitting our heads against a brick wall. We can't get moving financially and workwise.' They attributed this failure partly to their own lack of management expertise; for example, an inability to analyse costings properly:

We lack the know-how ... we might have the skills on machines but we haven't got the skills on the management side.

As the women were well aware, this made them vulnerable to exploitation by contractors:

You're completely at everybody's mercy ... if anyone comes in with some work you grab it, but you're going to be *exploited*.

However, they were still puzzled that 'the right type of work' was not forthcoming—that is, work that paid well. From her vantage point as director, Nancy could see that while they remained wholly dependent on contract work, financial crises would continue to recur. The alternative, as she perceived it, was for the enterprise to develop its own product, but there was no financial backing for such a venture. The other founding members could not understand why they were working so hard and earning so little; their only recourse was to blame either Nancy for bad management, or the rest of the women for not working as hard as themselves. Despite their close involvement with the running of the co-operative, they could not see beyond themselves, to the wider economic context, for an explanation of its non-viability. The women who joined later were even less able to understand, because of their restricted access to information, about the co-operative's finances. While also citing bad management as a factor, they still expressed genuine bewilderment about the cause of the factory's failure.

To summarise, the experience of working in the co-operative had, for at least some of the women, extended their conception of what was possible. They had realised their potential for actively taking control of their own work situation. But the knowledge thus gained did not extend beyond these particular circumstances to a broader social understanding of their position; they were unable to grasp the essential hopelessness of their economic predicament. This they could only interpret in terms of their own incompetence, as they lacked the resources to do otherwise.

Making contact with other workers in similar situations would at least have been a way out of their isolation. The means by which workers are able to foster an appreciation of the class nature of their struggle is often the trade union movement, the traditional resource of the working class. Without this resource, workers are cut off from the possibility of perceiving their common interests, especially those who are geographically isolated. Clearly, the organisation to which the Fakenham women would initially turn for advice and help in making such links and developing a broader strategy was their trade union. What follows, then, is a consideration of the role of trade unions in the Fakenham struggle.

The Union—paying dues for disenchantment

All the women at Fakenham Enterprises were members of a trade union, as pointed out earlier. Apart from Nancy, who was a member of ASTMS, they belonged to NUFLAT. They had joined the union for pragmatic, rather than political reasons. In a general sense, trade union membership may be regarded as an indicator of working-class consciousness. However, membership itself does not tell us much about an individual's political orientation. We also need to know both the character of the union, and the circumstances in which the person has joined.

The women who participated in the Fakenham occupation had all been union members at the time, and continued their membership while working in the co-operative. The women who joined the co-operative later almost all said that they had joined the union in order to attract shoe contracts from other unionised factories. Many described how they had been visited by two union representatives from Norwich, who had assured them that it was in the best interests of the enterprise for them to join the union. The implication was that the union would exercise its influence to obtain work for Fakenham. Despite its recruitment success, the union never had much presence in the factory. No union meetings were held there and most of the women said that they would not go, even if they were. Their interest went no further than payment of the dues and a hope that the union would find them further contracts.

None of the women felt that they had gained anything, as individuals, by belonging to NUFLAT. Neither did they think that the union had helped Fakenham. A few conceded that perhaps the union had been instrumental in obtaining work for the factory. But no-one knew of any specific contract which had resulted directly from the union's efforts. Their status as a unionised factory merely ensured that work would not be withheld by other unionised factories.

We need to consider whether the women's indifference and passivity in relation to the union was a reasonable response to their treatment by NUFLAT. Clearly, NUFLAT's behaviour formed part of their work experience and it was on this basis that their views developed. In fact, NUFLAT did nothing for them—the union officials took neither the women nor the co-operative seriously. Their reaction to the occupation, derision of the 'silly girls', has already been noted in Chapter 3. Far from offering any financial support, they refused to recognise the action and denied the women strike pay. Furthermore, they actually discouraged both their own members and the local trades council from contributing funds to the occupation. After the establishment of the co-operative, union activity was limited to an occasional visit by a union representative to collect dues; these men rarely talked to the women on the shop floor or spent any time in the factory.

What the union did or failed to do must be measured against what it could legitimately be expected to do. At the very least, a union might be expected to provide information about both seasonal fluctuations and the long-term contraction in the shoe industry, so that the enterprise could plan for changes in the volume of work. It may seem that the seasonal pattern should have been obvious to the women, but they failed to make the connection between the enterprise's recurrent crises, caused by the lack of contracts, and the seasonal demand shifts in the industry. The union might also be expected to seek publicity and raise political support from other unions, as well as lobbying the government directly for financial aid for industrial co-operatives. In failing to provide such support, let alone encouragement, NUFLAT was not atypical. Unfortunately, it shared with other unions a lack of experience in the practices of industrial democracy. Neither have trade unions developed the skills to enable them to provide technical expertise and advice to co-operatives. NUFLAT's inability to act effectively for the Fakenham co-operative was exacerbated by its location in a declining sector. A narrowly defensive response was all it could muster: negotiating 'good' redundancy payments and appealing to the government for import controls on shoes.

In the absence of a conventional management structure, it was not clear on what basis the workers should organise to protect their interests *within* the workplace. Both the women and the union were accustomed to dealing with an employer, and were confused by the lack of one. It was predictable that at least some of the women and union officials would come to see Nancy as the employer. This was reflected in some of the women's attitudes, as exemplified by Olive, who saw the union's role as representing the workers against Nancy.

> The union should stick up for the workers—demand the union rate. We don't get the rates of pay we should get and when the union man was here he told Nancy to make sure she paid us our holiday money. ... The union fights for the workers against management—I think of Nancy as the management.

As well as highlighting Olive's own view, this comment illustrates the union official's failure to grasp that the factory was a worker co-operative. Unable to assume a conventional role, the union had no role at all within the enterprise. The women's disenchantment with it was, therefore, hardly surprising.

Of the Fakenham women, only Edna, the union representative, did not explain her membership of NUFLAT in terms of an attempt to attract shoe contracts. None of the others expressed any identification with the union, or volunteered any comments on the general significance of the trade union movement as a whole. Edna had joined because she was 'aware that women weren't taking enough interest in things ... The trade unions are geared to men and are mainly run by men—that's been largely women's fault because they aren't interested.' Indeed, over half the women thought it was more important for men to be union members, 'because men are the breadwinners'. Only Nancy, Pat and Brenda thought that it was equally important for women to be in a union. Nonetheless, most agreed with Edna that unions were primarily geared towards men.

The Fakenham women were as ready as anyone else to
mouth clichés about unions having too much power,
unions causing strikes and unions being to blame for
inflation. Even Nancy, with her history of involvement in
industrial action, believed that: 'Britain is going downhill.
How can we survive with so many strikes that cost millions
of pounds?' On the other hand, nearly all the women
agreed with the views expressed by their husbands, that
'workers need strong unions to fight for their interests' and
that 'unions should try to get the workers a say in
management'. Such a view was somewhat ironic, given
that the women were their own managers at the co-
operative; and clearly their husbands did not recognise this.
A few of the women did feel that unions had no role to play
within co-operatives: 'you can't be self-employed like in a
co-operative and still demand union rates for the work . . .
You've got to share the losses as well as the gains'. These
inconsistencies, inherent in most workers' attitudes, have
been documented elsewhere (Mann, 1970). Typically,
inconsistency also characterises more general political
attitudes, as we shall now go on to see.

Opinions about 'Politics'

The Fakenham women, on the whole, voted Conservative.
One woman, for example, favoured 'the Conservative
Party's basic principles, like working and earning. People
should work and save and help themselves and not rely on
the state to help them.' Others echoed this view, believing
that 'every individual should sink or swim by his own
efforts and not ride on the backs of those who have the
ability to get on in life'. Only a few women voted Labour
'like my father always did', while a few were floating voters.
Two of the women never voted. The only person whose
voting behaviour had been affected by her experiences
during the occupation was Edna, as will be related below.
   According to a standard scale developed by Jessop in
1974 for measuring conservatism/deference, the women

emerged as highly conservative. Most approved of the royal family and public schools, opposed nationalisation and disagreed with the suggestion that 'the landed aristocracy should lose their land and privileges'. Perhaps this last question was of some relevance to their lives, in contrast to most of them, which were meaningless to the women; several women expanded their views on this, along the lines that 'we need the rich because they give the poor work'. Although in general the women did not identify with the working class or the labour movement, two-thirds did express a preference for a working-class Prime Minister. This, therefore, included many of the Conservative voters. They all gave very similar reasons, such as, 'he'd be one of us', 'he has more experience of how we live' and 'he would know the problems that face a working-class family'. Believing that neither party represented working people, they were almost unanimous in asserting that it made no difference which political party was in power.

The significance of their voting behaviour and of the attitudes expressed in response to opinion survey questions is, however, a highly contentious issue. An exclusive emphasis on these attitudes would suggest that the Fakenham women could be regarded simply as 'deferential'. Certainly, to the extent that they did discuss politics, they voiced clichés with the conventional dose of deference. However, it would be more accurate to stress the low salience of their political attitudes. Natalia's statement that she didn't believe in politics was echoed by many of the women. With the exception of some of the founding members of the co-operative, they rarely discussed politics. The Fakenham women, in sum, could be characterised as apolitical in the sence of conventional political commitment, rather than as actively embracing a deferential political ideology.

Not all the women shared in the general apathy, and to illustrate the possibilities of a more active consciousness, a couple of more detailed political portraits will be sketched. Nancy and Edna, who are described below, were in no way typical of the Fakenham workforce. Rather, they were the most politically conscious and frequently discussed politics.

In this way they serve as limiting-case examples, compared to the largely apathetic Fakenham workers. Both were central to the whole Fakenham struggle and, significantly, both had previous experience of industrial action. Despite this common ground, their general political orientations were quite different, as will become clear.

Nancy was a director of Fakenham Enterprises throughout its existence and had played a leading role in the occupation in 1972. Indeed, without her, the occupation would probably never have taken place. This was not, however, Nancy's first experience of workplace militancy. As mentioned in Chapter 5, she had organised a short but successful strike of Irish workers before she started working at Sextons, where she became a shop steward.

Although unable to account fully for her party allegiance, Nancy always voted Conservative, as did her husband. 'I'm Conservative-minded at heart,' she said, 'although in a sense it seems totally opposed to everything I've done. . . . I can't explain it to myself, but I could no more go out and vote Labour than I could not vote at all. I haven't ever been able to rationalise it, why it should be so, because I loathe Margaret Thatcher as a person.' She grew up in a predominantly Conservative area of Ireland and her parents voted Conservative. Still a practising Catholic, Nancy was on the committee of the local Catholic Women's League.

Her attitude towards the Labour Party, and party politics in general, was inconsistent. She had often attended ICOM meetings on behalf of the factory and knew that it had strong links with the Labour Party. On the one hand, she believed that:

> this country is in chaos because of excess profits . . . people
> don't realise that most of the wealth in England is owned by
> seven companies,

while on the other she often attributed England's problems to a lack of firm leadership, which the Conservative Party could remedy. In a different vein, she would say that all political parties were the same and 'it was people themselves that had to change'. A Conservative voter who attributed Labour's weakness to 'too much disunity and too much Communist policies', Nancy nevertheless considered that 'if there was ever real Communism, that would be good'. While committed to democratisation of the workplace, Nancy did not connect this goal with the kind of political context which might be conducive to these changes. Though critical of many aspects of the existing system, which 'they call free enterprise', she had little conception of an alternative to it.

If Nancy's general political orientations seem largely unaffected by her involvement in the Fakenham struggle, the reverse was true of Edna. She and her husband were longstanding union members. In 1971, the year before the Fakenham occupation, Edna had provided both financial and moral support for her husband during the three months he was on strike from the Post Office. Before the strike, Edna used to vote Conservative 'like my family voted before me', even though her husband always voted Labour. 'This is traditionally a Tory area,' she said, 'farm labourers are still scared of their bosses and so vote Tory like their bosses.' Edna now voted for the Labour Party. Although she had changed her voting pattern after the Post Office strike, an experience during the Fakenham occupation, a year later, had reinforced her decision.

> During the sit-in, the Tory M.P. (who I'd voted for) came to the factory and told me that nobody had a right to a job. I told him that everyone has a right to human dignity and, therefore, to a job so that he can support himself. And that I'd never vote for him again. Since then I've always voted Labour.

While working at the co-operative, Edna became shop steward and identified closely with the trade-union movement and the working class; she believed that 'the people of the country should have the wealth of the country'. However, she was critical of both trade unions and the Labour Party for not concerning themselves enough with the interests of working women. In particular, she was conscious of the discrimination suffered by married women:

> There's supposed to be equal rights, but it's not equal, because a married woman is still a second class citizen—like, you go on unemployment benefit, you pay the same stamp, but you get less money.

At shopfloor meetings Edna was one of the most vocal women, and was aware that, on the whole, women lacked the education and self-confidence to participate fully and put their questions and opinions. Such reticence was very obvious and posed a problem in the attempt to run the co-operative through open and collective discussion. Through her involvement in all-women's struggle, Edna's under-standing of the constraints operating on women had developed considerably further than her understanding of those operating on the working class as a whole.

Although Edna's political consciousness was, in fact, influenced by her experiences both before and during the co-operative, it would be mistaken to assume that a person's political attitudes can simply be deduced from a knowledge of their industrial history. This is borne out by our earlier discussion of the other women at the factory and by the portrait of Nancy. Despite their involvement in a highly unusual industrial set-up, apparently providing them with scope for political development, they remained largely unchanged. Although Fakenham Enterprises was an atypical workplace, the women's general political orient-ations were indistinguishable from those prevailing among the rural working class in the area. This can be substantiated by a consideration of the similarity between the women's political attitudes and those of their husbands. These men had no experience of working in a co-operative, nor had they shared their wives' experience to any significant degree. Thus, they may serve as a sample of typical working-class men in the area.

In general, the women were no more 'conservative' than

their husbands. Apart from the husbands greater tendency to apportion blame for strikes equally between unions and management, they expressed a mix of inconsistent and deferential attitudes similar to that of their wives. Their voting behaviour was much the same, as were their views on the power of unions, the merits of nationalisation and so on. Like their wives, they rarely discussed political issues and their ideological position had low salience in their images of society. The women's images of society were not just similar to their husbands'; they were also typical of those held by male agricultural workers in the adjoining county of Suffolk.[1] In conclusion, then, the political opinions of both the Fakenham women and their husbands were no different from those of other people living in the area.

Opinions about Gender

The Fakenham women were subordinate not only as members of the working class but also as women. In this field, too, their spoken opinions tended to accept and justify their subordination rather than challenge it. In the context of the factory this dimension was expressed in the wish, often voiced by the women, to hire a *man* as manager:

> Men seem to have a firmer hand in business than women. I haven't had a lot of opportunity to work for women, but men always seem to know what they're talking about. . . . When a man tells you what to do, you take more notice.

These views were commonly expressed as part of the tendency to lose hope in the co-operative and revert to a traditionally organised business.

As pointed out earlier, the women tended to blame the enterprise's failure on Nancy's bad management rather than wider economic circumstances. The immediate solution, in their eyes, was to hire a male manager. Their view that men, in general, made better managers than women, had

been reinforced by their experience of Nancy's management. For all of them, it was their only experience of a
female manager, so the equation between female and
unsuccessful management was an easy one to make.
Although this was never made explicit, the women
doubtless had in mind a typical middle-class manager, who
would indeed be male. Many of the women shared the view
that:

> If a man came into Fakenham Enterprises next week and ran
> it, it would be successful, because there's people at that
> factory that won't do what Nancy says. People won't argue
> with a man, but they will with women.

This view was held despite the fact that Hicks had been very
unpopular with the women when manager—because, as a
conventional middle-class manager, he was unsympathetic
to the problems of running a co-operative and treated the
workers with some disdain. Some of the women had joined
the factory after Hicks' departure, but for the most part
their attitudes, rather than being related to Hicks as such,
reflected stereotypes that were not amenable to isolated
countervailing examples. Be that as it may, in the absence
of effective organisation at the co-operative, women's pro-
pensity to defer to men was seen as a positive reason for
introducing the authority of a male manager. The women
also recognised the genuine problem that 'contractors come
to Fakenham Enterprises and see that we're only women,
and they take advantage of us'. Knowing that 'a man listens
to another man', the women were convinced that a male
manager could negotiate more profitable business deals.
(What the women omitted to mention was that as a wholly
working-class venture they were inevitably vulnerable to
such exploitation.)

Only Nancy saw it as a positive advantage to be a woman
manager in an all-women's enterprise. She worried that the
other women, lacking confidence in themselves, would
look to a man to resolve all their difficulties. 'Women tend
to defer to men,' she said, 'because it's been accepted for so

long that men are the dominant people. Men are the
managers, but women make just as good managerial
material.' Nancy implied that the Fakenham women were
inclined to endorse the moral order which legitimated their
own sexual subordination. However, it would be wrong to
infer that the attitudes illustrated above constitute moral
judgements about men's superiority. Rather, the women
were acknowledging existing sexual divisions in society.
Edna, for example, saw that men were placed differently in
the social order, such that they could develop their skills and
competence:

> Men are better managers now because women have never
> had the chance to get the experience. But a woman could be
> just as good as a man.

The women were inhibited not by an abstract approval of
men's authority, but by a sense that men were genuinely
better equipped to run a business.

This attitude was reinforced by the husbands of those
involved, who were sceptical of the co-operative's chances
of success. Brenda, for example, when arguing the need for
a male manager, declared: 'that's what my husband has been
saying for weeks—if we had a man we'd be on our feet'. As
the women were so clearly influenced by the views of their
husbands, we need to look not only at the workers but also
at their husbands' views of the Fakenham co-operative. I
have stressed the importance of considering the relationships between wives and husbands within the family, rather
than seeing women in isolation. The marital relationship
can be characterised as involving the exercise of traditional
authority by husbands over wives (Bell and Newby, 1976).
This is not meant to imply that women defer to men at all
times, but that marital interaction involves the negotiation
of a deferential relationship. Looking at the attitudes of
women who defer is not sufficient. It is necessary to take
account of those towards whom deference is expressed. The
experience of power negotiations with their husbands
forms part of the context in which the women gain their

understandings. The Fakenham women's deferential relation to men was maintained and reinforced at every point
by their husbands, as the following data illustrate.

Before discussing the husbands' views of the Fakenham
co-operative, their ideas about co-operatives in general
should be outlined. First, it must be said that some had no
understanding of co-operatives at all. Of the rest, there
were roughly two types of responses. Those who said they
would prefer to work for a co-operative gave purely instrumental reasons. They thought it simply meant sharing
the profits and of this they approved. The others, who had
no desire to work for a co-operative, gave reasons like the
following:

> I'd rather work for private enterprise because I know who
> my governor is. In a co-operative, you never actually know
> who you're working for.

Apart from the opportunity to share profits, none of the
husbands therefore saw any positive advantages to working
in a co-operative.

Not surprisingly, then, few of the husbands were sympathetic towards Fakenham Enterprises. They had neither
shared nor been touched by their wives' experience of
participating in a co-operative workplace; only Edna's
husband actively gave support. Instead, they were angered
by the women's failure to provide a regular and adequate
income. Over the years, this had caused considerable
tension between wives and husbands, so that many of the
women were scared to return home when wages were poor
or non-existent. Husbands also complained about the long
hours that some of the women had worked and their
tendency to 'bring their worries home from work'. Overall,
husbands were constantly critical of the co-operative, with
the result that in the presence of their husbands, most of the
women were defensive about working there.

The husbands identified bad management as the cause of
Fakenham's low pay. Like the women, they could not see
beyond the enterprise for an explanation of the co-

operative's difficulties. 'There's no discipline, too many chiefs and not enough Indians,' one husband complained, 'people come and go as they please. The should clock in and out.' From here it was a short step to thinking that:

> Fakenham Enterprises needs a bloke. Women won't look up to other women. They'd work harder if a man was boss.

Thus, the introduction of a male manager was commonly held to be the solution to the firm's problems. This was not because they understood these difficulties, but rather because of their prejudices about women's capacities; for most of the husbands a good manager was, by definition, male. As one husband said disparagingly: 'women are too temperamental, men are stricter. You need a man to give orders and be listened to.' But though they said 'a man', actually not *any* man would do. From the rest of their remarks, it was clear that the type of male manager they had in mind would be of a different social class to themelves. At no point did the husbands indicate a willingness to take on a managerial role themselves; being male was not in itself an adequate qualification.

The husbands' negative response to the women's attempt to control their own work situation must have undermined the women's self-confidence. Having a different conception of the co-operative from their wives, they certainly did not encourage them to participate in it more fully. They would not have been willing to accept the reduction in the time spent on domestic work that this would have entailed. The fact that there were no men at the factory itself was of central importance. Given that most of the women had deferential attitudes towards men, their efforts to take control might not have been possible in the first place but for this factor. The absence of male workers enabled some of the women to take on leadership roles and responsibility in the co-operative. Authority structures within this all-women's factory were transformed, but those within the family remained intact. The women's new-found strength within the workplace did not threaten the traditional patterns of domination between wives and husbands. On the contrary, whenever the women were demoralised at work, and looked to the family for support, they were confronted with the hostility of their husbands. In the face of such opposition in the home, the Fakenham women were remarkably steadfast in their efforts to keep the co-operative alive.

Consciousness

The Fakenham women were doubly oppressed—as women and as workers—and yet they seem to subscribe to opinions which justify their oppression. What are we to make of this?

First, it must be said that they are by no means unusual in this. Their husbands' images of society were similar to their own; and as I have pointed out, those images closely resembled those held by male agricultural workers elsewhere. More generally, it is very commonly found that people in subordinate positions in society seem to say things that imply acceptance of (or at least lack of opposition to) their subordination. Many manual workers, for example, vote Conservative; they give their electoral support to a party committed to a social and economic system in which they remain at the bottom. Women in situations far worse than those of the Fakenham women will say that it is somehow 'natural' and 'right' that men should dominate.

So one of the major problems for anyone interested in people's ideas about society and their position in it—interested in their consciousness—is to explain why people seem to subscribe to beliefs that imply their subordination. The problem is both crucial and difficult. Crucial, because here we have a major mechanism by which oppressive societies remain stable. Difficult, because the traditional solution to the problem is untenable.

That traditional solution hinges on the notion of 'false consciousness'. The notion claims to be both a description and an explanation. What it claims to describe is a situation in which people have the 'wrong' ideas—wrong in the sense

that they are not 'in their interests'. A worker who supports,
and votes for, the Conservative Party is thinking and doing
something that is against her or his class interests. A woman
who believes that men are naturally better managers is
subscribing to a belief that is against the interests of women
as a sex.

The explanation embedded in the notion of 'false consciousness' has been called the 'dominant ideology thesis'. It
assumes that there is: 'a set of beliefs which dominates all
others and which, through its incorporation in the consciousness of subordinate classes, tends to inhibit the
development of radical political dissent' (Abercrombie and
Turner, 1978:149). Those who benefit from the subordination of workers or women (i.e. capitalists or men)
promote ideas that justify this subordination (the 'ideology'). Because they have the upper hand in society they
have all sorts of resources open to them to do this, from
control of schooling and the media to greater prestige and
greater access. Their ideas are thus more powerful than any
opposing ideas—they constitute the 'dominant ideology'.
This dominant ideology gets inside the heads of those who
are in subordinate positions: women, workers, or whoever.
They then accept their subordination because their ideas
imply that it is legitimate.

'False consciousness' and 'dominant ideology' are terms
coined within Marxism. But the form of explanation they
imply stretches far wider. Mainstream sociologists also
make much use of it. For example, the concept of
'deference' has been taken as the supreme example of 'false'
consciousness.[2] In feminist writing, too, it is perhaps the
most common way of explaining why women accept their
subordination to men.

Obviously, it is a form of explanation with a great deal of
intuitive plausibility. But empirical research in recent years
has cast doubt on it in at least two ways.

First, the explanation implies that those in subordinate
positions carry around in their heads a *fixed* and *coherent* set
of ideas. But whether people do carry round such a set of
ideas is highly dubious. Recent empirical research on

manual workers denies that workers share a coherent system of beliefs of *any* kind, and characterises working-class consciousness as 'inconsistent', 'contradictory', 'fragmented', 'ambivalent', 'inchoate' and 'conflicting'.[3] Although these writers differ in their emphasis, all agree in rejecting the 'dominant ideology thesis' in favour of an account of British working-class culture which stresses its *dualistic* character.

The 'dominant ideology thesis', with its insistence on the fixity and coherence of particular workers' beliefs, cannot readily provide an explanation of the militant action undertaken by supposedly 'deferential' workers during what became known as the British 'strike explosion' of the 1960s. How could workers with a set of supposedly 'false deferential' attitudes suddenly stage a dramatic strike or a factory occupation? To account for such 'spontaneous' outbursts of industrial unrest, Mann (1973) extended the theory of dual consciousness, by suggesting that an 'oppositional' consciousness, which normally co-exists with the dominant ideology, is mobilized in times of conflict. Given the 'profound dualism' in workers' consciousness, combining a passive sense of alienation with unmistakeable signs of conscious deprivation, their compliance is never more than 'pragmatic'. In a specific situation of conflict, such as a strike, the normally 'latent' hostility may be brought to the surface in an 'explosion' of consciousness. But Mann thought it a mistake to view such outbursts as part of a *cumulative* process, whereby formerly 'latent' hostility would finally be turned into revolutionary class consciousness:

> 'Explosion' is an apt metaphor—it bangs but it cannot build (1973:51).

The militant activity is typically transient, rarely resulting in any enduring revision of consciousness.

In the case of Fakenham, the formation of the co-operative meant that it was not a case of transient militancy followed by a return to normal. But even if the women who occupied the Fakenham factory did so in a moment of genuine radicalism, their experiences certainly neither dislodged their underlying adherence to a 'deferential' and conservative ideology at the abstract level, nor transformed their attitudes at the concrete level. What is not clear is whether there is any evidence apart from the occupation itself for even a temporary 'explosion' of consciousness.

Indeed, Mann (1970) has suggested that it is the very diversity of possible responses to the status quo which helps to stabilise it. Typically, workers' ideas about society have two poles, not one. At the abstract political level, remote from their day–to–day experience, people adhere to 'dominant' values; at the level of concrete experience, support for 'deviant' values is stronger. From this Mann concluded that the compliance of the subordinate classes results from the duality of their consciousness. Insofar as it is possible to distinguish between 'dominant' and 'subordinate' conceptions of society, the majority of workers are not exclusively bound to one *or* the other, but somehow fluctuate between them.

There is thus a split between *two* levels of consciousness, the abstract and the situational. Attitudinal studies which rely solely on questions posed in general terms are almost bound to discover a 'consensus' framed in terms of the 'dominant' value-system. Studies which specify particular social contexts will discover *another* 'consensus', framed in terms of the 'subordinate' value-system.

This would seem to explain the typical case of someone who will agree to such abstract assertions as 'unofficial strikes are ruining the country', but will themselves, in the pressure of a particular situation, take unofficial strike action. This very split is stabilising, in that the lessons of concrete experience are not translated to the more general level, and do not become part of an overall critique of society. In a similar way—though there has been much less work on the question—the argument has seemed persuasive to socialist feminists who have found in dual consciousness an explanation of the apparently contradictory nature of women's consciousness with regard to male domination.[4] So, as far as the Fakenham women were concerned, their knowledge that Hicks had been incompetent did not disturb their belief that, in general, men made the best managers.

The idea of dual consciousness represents an advance on explanations of working–class quiescence couched in terms of the deprived endorsing their deprivation. Nevertheless, according to this idea, compliance is still perceived to be the result of a dominant value system in combination with, and serving to maintain, a deficiency of understanding on the part of the working class. This would equally apply to several of the ways in which women's compliance with male domination has been accounted for. The conception of dual consciousness, then, can be criticised for its undue concern (which it shares with the dominant ideology thesis) with people's attitudes and values, and its consequent failure to deal adequately with people's social and practical experience.[5] Returning to the example above, the women's belief that managers should be male reflects their predominant experience of managerial positions being occupied by men; it was part of their knowledge of the world rather than an abstract moral stance. It has been argued that as a result of the experience of domination and powerlessness, the deprived perceive their social subordination not in moral terms, but as a fact of life, 'natural' and inevitable. The dual consciousness theory does not deal adequately with how people's ideas about the system and conceptions of alternatives to it are constructed. According to one author, the *experience* of constraint, the inability to exercise control over one's own life, is crucial to the development of:

> a mode of thought which involves a relatively unreflected, passive view of the world determining, rather than being determined by, the individual (Prandy, 1979:466).

The deprived have conceptions of the social world which reflect their experience of external constraints. These constraints impinge as facts of existence about which there appears to be no question of exercising one's will. People have an (at least partially) accurate understanding of the conditions of their existence and perceive there to be very limited possibilities for change in them. As Prandy puts it: 'those who exercise least control over their lives are most likely to adopt an attitude towards society of its natural "givenness" ' (ibid., 450). This is particularly significant for women, whose subordination is generally legitimated in biological terms.

One interesting result to emerge from Prandy's data is the tendency of individuals to blame other individuals, rather than 'the system'. To blame the system would require them to perceive an alternative to it. Without this perception, the apparent necessity of the given social order leads them to attach blame in relation to only a very limited number of issues. Moral issues arise only when people see themselves or others as able to modify existing practices. For example, workers may perceive that relations of dependence on and subordination to management are inherent in any advanced economic system. However, there are occasions when particular managements and particular practices are not perceived as inevitable products of the system. Particular managements may then be seen as 'good' or 'bad' without this implying a moral evaluation of the overall system of managerial authority.

From the account given of the problems faced by the Fakenham co-operative, it is clear that most did not lie within the women's control. Part of a declining industry and set up in the wake of a business failure, Fakenham Enterprises existed in a harsh economic environment. Launched with inadequate finance, it also suffered from a lack of both managerial skills and a regular flow of orders. And the women simply did not have the capital to develop their own product. They were unable to surmount these obstacles; it is doubtful whether any other workers in similar circumstances could have done so. The factors affecting the women's understanding of the restrictions on them and their enterprise are summarised below.

First, situated as they were in a remote rural community characterised by little geographical mobility, the Fakenham

women had a narrow range of social experience. They
remained largely cut off, socially and physically, from other
sections of society—their world was Fakenham. Their
encapsulation within a social system providing them with
few alternative conceptions of what was possible and
desirable militated against any change in their political
orientations. Secondly, the workers were cut off from the
trade union movement, and thereby from other workers,
both locally and nationally. Although all the women were
union members they received virtually no assistance as a
consequence. Not only did the union officials treat the
women with contempt, they also hindered their attempts to
gain support from the wider union movement. Thirdly,
apart from a few random visits by political activists, the
women lacked the opportunity to connect with a political
culture that might have broadened their horizons and
provided some support. The only visible sign of a political
party in Fakenham was the Conservative social club.

These problems were all exacerbated by the fact that the
Fakenham workers were women. Not only were they subject to the conditions of the rural working class but also,
being women, they were structurally located in another
distinct set of relations of subordination—that of women to
men. As a result of the class-gender system, women are the
most exploited members of the working class. Their experience of employment makes them especially unsuitable
for running a co-operative. Women generally work in low
grade jobs, and have little scope for developing the managerial skills necessary for running a business and organising
their own workplace. Unskilled male members of the working class would, admittedly, hardly be better equipped to
run a co-operative. But, women are subject to further constraints arising from the domestic duties that they must
perform in the home.

As we have seen, the domestic life-cycle has particularly
important consequences for women's work and largely
determines the extent to which they can become involved in
the workplace. The effect on the Fakenham co-operative
was double-edged. On the one hand, women with school-

age children could only work part-time, thus limiting their opportunity for participation in the co-operative. On the other hand, the women with no dependent children could afford to work for fluctuating and uncertain wages, as the actual amount of money earned was less crucial to their households. In this sense, perhaps, the co-operative survived as long as it did because women are secondary wage-earners at specific stages of the life-cycle.

Because there were no male workers in the factory the women could more easily take the initiative to assume control of their workplace. But the co-operative existed in a male economic environment and the women had to deal with overbearing middle-class men as managers, directors and customers. In addition, when looking beyond the enterprise, they were quickly undermined. They were confronted with a predominantly male trade union movement and political culture, as well as with their husbands, most of whom were unsympathetic to the women's involvement in Fakenham Enterprises. Offsetting this to some extent was the advantage that, in a small all-women's factory, they could form strong friendship bonds with each other.

The conditions in which the occupation took place and in which the co-operative functioned were such as to minimise the political impact on the people involved. The militancy experienced by the women during the occupation was in no way reinforced; it was for most of them their first taste of industrial action and an almost unprecedented event for Fakenham. In the absence of local support, making connections between their own particular struggle and wider industrial and political struggles was an urgent need, but their isolation made this extremely difficult.

The experience of working in a co-operative did not transform the Fakenham women's political orientations at the societal level. Neither did it have major repercussions on the sexually based division of labour in their homes. The organisation of their family lives was untouched by the women's involvement in and commitment to a co-operative workplace, regardless of their varying degrees of involvement with the enterprise. For many of the women, who joined the co-operative subsequent to its establishment and worked on a part-time basis, working in a co-operative was not felt to be qualitatively different from their previous experience of employment. To them, it was a job like any other. It is not surprising, then, that working at Fakenham Enterprises had no ramifications for their political consciousness or domestic lives. This was more surprising in the case of the women who were strongly identified with the co-operative, having set it up themselves. At the level of the enterprise, these women were active and innovative, introducing and sustaining collective work practices and assuming new responsibilities. But the increased confidence and knowledge they gained through these activities never found expression beyond the confines of the factory.

The co-operative's ultimate demise left the women embittered and pessimistic about the possibilities for change. Whatever the potential for political radicalisation in a worker-controlled enterprise, a failed attempt of this kind may actually increase workers' sense of powerlessness. Having fought to take control over their workplace, and having seen that attempt fail, the Fakenham women experienced more intensely the apparent inevitability of the capitalist system. In a dramatic way this serves as an illustration of much working-class experience, in which real and ideological constraints interact to reproduce powerlessness.

Postscript:
Co-operatives in the 1980s

The period which saw the rise and fall of Fakenham Enterprises already seems a long time ago. Since then a Conservative Government has presided over a dramatic increase in unemployment to which there has been little effective resistance by the labour movement. Yet even then the frequency of factory closures was frightening. Fakenham Enterprises was the product of a wave of industrial militancy that characterised those early years of recession. From the perspective of the mid-1980s we may wonder whether there is anything to be learnt from that and similar episodes. The contemporary resurgence of interest in producer co-operatives makes this a pertinent question.

An enthusiasm for co-operatives has developed for the most pressing of reasons and the best of motives. But in terms of job creation and preservation the record of co-operatives is undeniably poor (Thornley, 1981 : 111). It is never pleasant to have to cast a shadow over an optimistic view. Unfortunately that is what I have to do. Co-operatives are not a panacea. Naively embarked upon, they cannot provide more than a temporary alternative, and are as likely to inhibit as to develop consciousness.

Considering how little impact co-operatives have made on any sector of the economy, there has been a remarkable burgeoning over the last decade of organisations set up to promote co-operatives. Many and varied, these agencies are a phenomenon in themselves. Not only have new voluntary bodies sprung up, but state support for co-operatives has been growing. At the national level the Co-operative Development Agency was launched by an Act of Parliament in 1978. The Tories, Liberals and Labour Party all welcomed its establishment. It was to concentrate its efforts

183

on job creation by promoting industrial and service co-operatives. Over forty local Co-operative Development Agencies have since been set up to stimulate, or simulate, activity. Co-operatives have become popular too among local authorities, which have been forced to intervene more directly in their local economies to stem industrial decline. The Labour-controlled Greater London Council is a case in point. With the establishment of a Greater London Enter-prise Board co-operatives have become an integral part of its radical approach to the regeneration of industry and employment.

In the Labour Party nationally there has been renewed enthusiasm for worker co-operatives. A discussion docu-ment issued in 1980 heralds them as offering: 'a true socialist approach to economic planning and development'. It argues that support for workers' co-operatives today is particularly crucial in view of Britain's rapid deindustrial-isation and increasing unemployment! Although profit should not be the main motive of these so-called 'islands of socialism', it is made clear that they will have to be eco-nomically viable, i.e. they must produce a surplus. But why co-operatives should succeed when capitalists are finding it increasingly difficult to do so is a question not even asked, let alone answered.

Labour's endorsement of co-operatives for their socialist potential has not blinded the Conservative Party to their advantages for capital. As a means of increasing product-ivity and easing labour relations co-operatives can be promoted as furthering capitalist ends. The Tories see co-operatives as an alternative form of company in the small firm sector. In labour-intensive industries where the profit margin is low, small businesses in the shape of co-operatives can provide vital services for national and multinational companies. Co-operatives fit easily into Tory plans to restructure the economy according to the needs of capital: 'they provide a source of cheap, non-unionised "peri-pheral" labour which is an important supplement to the "central" workers located in the larger factories and offices' (Pelly, 1981). They also fit in all too well with the Tories' aim, enshrined in their self-help ideology, that *workers* should take responsibility for the realisation of profit. 'Having a stake in the business' is seen as the best incentive to work. From this perspective, co-operatives reinforce the equation of ownership and control.

Where the Labour Party most clearly parts company with the Conservatives or Liberals is in advocating that a future Labour Government would give workers in private firms the legislative right to convert their enterprises into workers' co-operatives by acquiring the assets. The most likely time for this demand to be voiced by workers is when their workplace is threatened with closure or when rationalisation resulting in job loss is being promoted. This is expressly recognised in the Party's discussion document. As it stands this sounds very like the policy Benn was following when he financed the formation of co-operatives at Meriden, Kirkby and the *Scottish Daily News*. As commercial ventures these co-operatives had enormous problems — the major one being that they were hopelessly undercapitalised from the start (see chapter 2). Raising capital is a particular problem for co-operatives because their rules specify that all the capital must be owned by worker-members. Unable to raise capital by having outside shareholders they are heavily dependent on state loans. Unless a future Labour Government was seriously committed to substantial state funding of worker co-operatives their legislative proposals might simply result in a proliferation of hopelessly lame ducks.

This is not meant to imply that co-operatives fail simply because they are co-operatives. Small businesses of any complexion face severe pressures. Today's economy is dominated by huge conglomerates which control distribution and marketing and consequently control all small firms. The struggling co-operative is too often compared with a hypothetical private firm which is efficient, capital-rich, using modern technology and steadily expanding through reinvestment. Small may be beautiful but it tends to be short-lived; the failure rate of small businesses is in reality very high.

Why, then, should working-class people want to take on the responsibility for the viability of the enterprises in which they work by setting up co-operatives? That this question is rarely asked is in itself significant— being symptomatic of a number of middle-class assumptions about the nature of work. In particular, implicit in leftist discussions about workers' co-operatives is the assumption that having responsibility at work is desirable in itself.

However, such enthusiasm as working-class people have shown for co-operatives is a pragmatic response to the prospect of poverty that unemployment entails. Acquiring greater control over the workplace would indeed advance the struggle for job security, decent wages and work conditions but *ownership* is not a necessary concomitant, nor even the best means of achieving it. In general workers do not have the confidence, the skills or the financial resources to want to take on the risks consequent on ownership of their workplaces. Although committed to full self-management, the Fakenham workers had to resort to hiring middle-class managers when faced with financial crises. There is nothing in co-operative ideals to challenge the capitalist distribution of skills on a class basis. Neither do they challenge the reproduction of the division of labour between the sexes.

In practice co-operatives do not even provide the decent wages and conditions that have been the object of so much working-class struggle. The survival of the Fakenham co-operative for as long as five years was attributable solely to the self-sacrifice of the women involved. In this it was not unusual. Few co-operatives have been commercially viable; most survive through the collective efforts of the work-force, who tolerate low pay, unpaid overtime, and poor working conditions. In conditions close to sweated labour, members of co-operatives spend much of their time worrying about how their individual enterprise, and with it their livelihood, will survive. Their predominant concerns reflect the characteristic problems of keeping a small business afloat.

The repercussions on home life constitute a considerable

strain—especially for women with a heavy domestic work-load. Women know what it is to work for love not money! Small wonder that, for the Fakenham women, forming a co-operative was the last resort. This was also the case more recently for the women at Lee Jeans. In 1981 they occupied their factory in Greenock, Scotland, for seven months to protest against closure. Although the formation of a co-operative was suggested to the women, they were extremely reluctant to take on the responsibility involved. In the event a new private owner came forward, which was the best outcome so far as the workforce was concerned. They wanted an end to their struggle, not a continuation of it.

In the mid-1980s fears have re-emerged that deepening economic recession will have a disproportionately severe effect on women's employment. Women face the prospect of a deterioration in the conditions of wage labour and, indeed, domestic labour. Co-operatives employ a high proportion of female labour in what are traditionally 'women's jobs'. The setting up of labour-intensive manu-facturing and service co-operatives, providing low paid and insecure jobs, only reproduces women's inferior position in the labour market.

Among socialists the interest in co-operatives is not merely an economic one centring on employment. It has become fashionable once more to see co-operatives as representing a 'prefigurative form', exemplifying a form of organisation within capitalism which anticipates socialism. Marx himself is quoted as having described producer co-operatives as demonstrating certain key tenets of socialism in practice. Even a recent study by the Wales TUC con-cludes that:

> Co-operatives are seen as preferable to any incoming firm in that they are prefigurative of a higher form or post-capitalist social organisation incorporating, as they do, social control, democratic management, the subordination of capital to labour and dependable employment . . . (Logan and Gregory, 1981:122).

By 'generating experience on the advantages of popular control' co-operatives are said to have an important role to play in the development of political consciousness.

This book has been an exploratory study of the consciousness of a group of workers who were engaged in an experiment in workers' control. I have argued that the formation of a worker co-operative cannot simply be taken as an indication of radical political consciousness. Co-operatives are set up for a number of reasons, ranging from ideological to more pragmatic ones, depending on the prevailing political circumstances and the consciousness and experience of the particular workers involved. Even within a single co-operative, the workers may have differing conceptions of it. The political impact of co-operatives is, then, an open question. Equally, it is impossible to construct a model of the type of political consciousness appropriate to their establishment.

I have stressed throughout that the effect on consciousness of involvement in a co-operative cannot be divorced from questions about commercial viability. If co-operatives are mostly doomed to financial collapse, or survival only at the workers' expense, then this is the economic reality which shapes people's experience of them. The Left's model of the type of co-operative which is potentially radicalising is one where working-class women and men demand control over their workplace, thereby challenging capitalists' power over labour. However it is precisely this type of co-operative which has typically failed to survive or has kept operating only at the expense of the workers' own pay and conditions. The ideals behind workers' co-operatives cannot compensate for the experience of defeat or self-exploitation of those involved, neither of which foster the development of political consciousness.

This is not to deny that the way in which work is organised in a co-operative may itself provide valuable experiments in workers' self-management—tasks may be rotated, pay differentials reduced or eradicated, democratic decision-making procedures instituted. But given the necessity for financial survival, anxiety about the firm's viability will dominate daily experience of working in the co-operative. In this context radical work practices do not have a radicalising effect on consciousness. Rather, shifting responsibility for a firm's viability onto the workers increases the potential for demoralisation because they will blame themselves for its failure.

On one thing it is necessary to be clear. The failure of Fakenham Enterprises—and of the co-operative movement more generally—does not arise from the failure of those who took part. In the conditions I have described the very attempt to establish control at workplace level is a triumph over adversity. The Fakenham women's overt political orientations were of far less importance than the fact that they took action. They gave other workers an example of an attempt, however short-lived, do democratise the workplace and resist redundancies. For women, too, it represented a demand for sexual equality at work and a refusal to be ignored by the trade union movement. In the event, they failed to achieve their goal. This indicates the strength of the forces with which they had to contend. The women themselves were not lacking in determination and courage.

Appendix A
The Shoe Industry in Decline

The number of pairs of shoes 'consumed' per head in Britain rose from 3.2 (1950) to 4.55 (1971) but then fell to 4.02 in 1975—a drop of 30 million pairs per annum (Bell, 1977). As consumer income rises, the proportion spent on footwear rises relatively less. The falling birth rate has also hit children's shoe sales: those of Clark's fell by 10 per cent to 9 million pairs by 1976/77 (Bell, 1977). In short, the market is diminishing.

In 1952, a mere 2.9 per cent of the shoes sold in Britain were imported; in 1976 the figure was 41.3 per cent (Bell, 1977). The industry is relatively labour-intensive—labour costs accounted for 61 per cent of net output in 1972, compared with 52 per cent for manufacturing as a whole. So it is particularly threatened by low wage manufacturers. As one manufacturer declared, 'shoes which I could not make for less than £4.50 arrived at the dock from Taipei at £1.85' (Bell, 1977).

In 1975, the recession hit especially hard: total British production fell by 10 per cent compared with the early 1970s; orders received were 25 per cent below those of 1973; deliveries were at their lowest level since the 1950s; exports were down 7 per cent on 1974; the proportion of imports rose.

All these pressures—competition, imports, recession—together with technical change, have resulted in declining employment. Employment in the British footwear industry reached a post-war peak of 127,000 in 1950, from which it had fallen to 77,900 in 1975. The rate of decline in numbers employed accelerated in the 1970s; 6,000 jobs in the industry were lost between June 1974 and June 1975

(Goodman *et al.*, 1977 : 52). This contraction in the labour force has been associated with a gradual change in its gender composition. Before World War II, the labour force was predominantly male; by 1975, the proportions were 56 per cent women and 44 per cent men. The number and propor- tion of men have fallen mainly because labour-saving technical changes over the past two decades have been concentrated in the male departments of shoe production.

There has been a general increase in the number of large establishments (employing over 1,000) in the industry, but the small and medium sized still accounted for a substantial share of sales and employment in 1972. Indeed, in terms of establishment numbers, it is the middle size that has declined in importance, while both large and small have increased. There are few economies of scale to be made in the shoe industry. This is because it produces a wide variety of shoes—over 10,000 different styles in any one year— with the styles changing from year to year, subject to the dictates of fashion. There is limited scope for long production runs. Pratten and Dean estimated that, in 1964, unit costs could not be greatly reduced at output levels above 1,400 pairs per day, and such production levels are attainable in the small range establishments (quoted in Goodman *et al.*, 1977 : 47). This book also contains a fuller account of the British footwear industry, from which I have drawn substantially .

A specific problem for small shoe manufacturers is the concentration of ownership of distribution outlets. The small firm owns no outlet, whereas the British Shoe Corporation owns 30 per cent of multiple shoe shops. The strategy of securing control of outlets is largely un- available to the small manufacturers because they cannot produce the necessary product range competitively. Thus the reliance of individual small enterprises on retail outlets for contracts makes them potentially vulnerable to a shortage of orders.

Appendix B
The Trade Union

Most manual workers in the British footwear manufacturing industry are organised by the National Union of
Footwear, Leather and Allied Trades. Before 1971, the shoe
union was known as the National Union of Boot and Shoe
Operatives. (For a comprehensive account of the union's
history, see Fox, 1958.) Since it merged with several smaller
unions in 1971, NUFLAT has also organised in the leather
producing, made-up leather goods and glove trades. In
addition, it organises, to a lesser extent, in footwear
repairing and components. Widening the field of recruitment has done little, however, to arrest the steady decline in
the union's membership in the post-war period, as may be
seen from Table 6.

Table 6 Membership of the National Union of Footwear,
Leather and Allied Trades

Year	Membership
1940	94,000
1950	87,000
1960	78,000
1970	63,000
1975	66,000★

★This includes approximately 11,000 members in the Leather Trade
Group.
Source: Goodman (1977:80).

The dramatic decline since 1940 is almost wholly
accounted for by the fall in the number of manual workers
employed in the industry. Contraction in membership has
largely affected men. In 1935, for example, only 35 per cent

of members were women. Now, women slightly out-number men. But this position is not reflected in the number of official positions women hold—virtually all national and branch officials are male.

NUFLAT's fortunes have been closely tied to those of the industry itself, and thus to those of the footwear employers. In particular, the nature of the product market, which is beset by uncertainty (i.e. seasonal, cyclical, fashion and other fluctuations), has limited the basis for a militant approach to collective bargaining. The union's industrial policy can be summed up as one of moderation—'peace', 'partnership' and 'productivity'. It is proud of its long record of peaceful coexistence with the employers. There has been virtually no expenditure on strike activity. (The amount of strike benefit paid out between 1949 and 1974 was approximately £2,100. See Goodman *et al.*, 1977:94.) The most recent official strike was in Leicester in 1940. The last official strike in Norwich occurred in 1897.

The late sixties and early seventies were characterised by an intensification of the process of decline, and an increasing incidence of redundancies, closures, short-time working, and unemployment. The union responded by focussing its attention on imports, which threaten the employers and union alike, and its 'solution' has been defined as that of lobbying the government to impose quotas and/or tariff barriers, so far with little success.

Notes and References

Chapter 1 *Work and the Family*

1. The discussion in this section is based on the following books: Fogarty, Rapoport and Rapoport (1971); Jephcott, Seear and Smith (1962); Klein (1965); Myrdal and Klein (1956); Rapoport and Rapoport (1971); and Yudkin and Holme (1963).

2. Referring to these books, Brown (1976:27) makes the same point:

> The largest category of studies of women *qua* women as employees is that which regards the employment of women as in some way giving rise to problems—for the women themselves in combining their two roles; for the employer in coping with higher rates of absence and labour turnover, and demands for part-time work; for the social services in providing for the care of children of working mothers, or in coping with the supposed results of maternal neglect; for husbands and other kin in taking over part of the roles of wife and mother; and even for the sociologist in attempting to discern the 'motivation' of women in paid employment.

3. The essential contribution which married women's earnings make to the family income has now been well documented. See Land (1981:13).

4. Siltanen (1981) provides a critical overview of these approaches to women's place in paid labour. See Blackburn and Mann (1979) for a detailed discussion of labour markets in general.

5. Oakley (1981) cites several studies, including her own, which suggest that the time spent on housework has actually risen with the invention of new household appliances.

6. A bibliography of the literature is contained in Kaluzynska (1980), who describes the increasingly scholastic debates that ensued about whether domestic labour produces surplus value. She also summarises the main criticisms—such as naive economism and functionalism.

7. For an extensive discussion of the ideology of the family and the cultural production of gender, see Barrett (1980).

8. For example, having clearly distinguished in the text between the different significance of paid work for the young girls and the

older married women, Pollert proceeds in her final chapter to talk about how wage labour creates the potential for *all* women to gain a new consciousness. Porter distinguishes two stages— before and after childbearing—but then ignores even these by going on to claim the typicality of her sample of married women with dependent children. They are *not* typical.

Whereas most studies of women workers have tended to be of professional and white-collar employees, these studies look at the distinctive features of working-class women in the work situation. For an extended review of these and other studies, see Wajcman (1982, 1981).

9. This 'job/gender' model is developed by Feldberg and Glenn (1979). An important exception is Beynon and Blackburn's study (1972) which does attempt, though not entirely successfully, to overcome the false separation between the conditions of work and family life for both women and men.

10. Cavendish (1981), Pollert (1981) and Porter (1982) similarly make statements about how 'all these women saw their primary focus as the home'.

11. Data supplied by the authors, Blackburn and Mann (1979). At the time that Myrdal and Klein were writing *Women's Two Roles,* Dubin (1956) was noting that almost three-quarters of American industrial workers did not see work as a central life interest.

12. This theme is the subject of an article by Purcell (1979) on the stereotype of the passive woman worker.

Chapter 2   *Co-operatives: an experiment in workers' control*

1. For a detailed survey of the ICOM companies, see Oakeshott (1978). For Scott Bader in particular, see Blum (1968).

2. The notion of ownership used by Scott Bader is a restricted one in that the employees are denied the right to dispose of their shares. For an interesting discussion of the concept of ownership, see Rose *et al.* (1976).

3. A full account of the formation of these three co-operatives can be found in Coates (1976).

4. Tomlinson (1980/81) has reviewed these responses to co-operatives. See also Thornley (1981).

5. For example, see Coates and Topham (1968, 1974); Coates (1965, 1968, 1976); and IWC pamphlets.

6. This is contrasted to 'workers' self-management' which indicates attempts to administer a socialised economy democratically. There is now an extensive literature on the Yugoslav system of worker–management; see, for example, the work of Vanek (1970, 1975).

7. See Hyman (1974) for a critical review of the publications of the IWC.

8. See Blumberg (1968) for a critique of Clegg's argument.

9. Their ambivalence found expression in the debate following the publication in 1977 of the *Report of the Committee of Inquiry on Industrial Democracy* (The Bullock Report). For a discussion of the Bullock Report's proposals, and reactions to it, see Moore (1977).

10. Cressey and MacInnes (1980) argue cogently that Marxists have failed to present an adequate theory of the relationship between capital and labour at the point of production, or the relationship between class struggle at the level of the factory and class struggle at the level of society as a whole.

11. An important exception is Eccles's book on Kirkby (1981).

12. Criticising this narrow demand for workers' control, Braverman (1974:445) suggests that:

> Without the return of the requisite technical knowledge to the mass of workers and reshaping of the organisation of labour . . . balloting within factories and offices does not alter the fact that the workers remain as dependent as before upon 'experts' . . . Thus genuine workers' control has as its prerequisite the demystifying of technology and the reorganisation of the mode of production.

Chapter 3   *Formation of the Fakenham Co-operative*

1. In East Anglia as a whole, two-thirds of the 380,000 men in full-time employment were in manual occupations and 60 per cent of male workers were earning less than the median earnings for Great Britain of £62. There were about 140,000 women in full-time employment of whom two-thirds were in non-manual occupations, with a further 90,000 women working part-time. The vast majority of these women were earning 2–3 per cent less than their equivalents in other regions.
Regional Economic Review, East Anglia Economic Planning Council, May 1977, Table A, p. 2; p. 4; Table C, p. 5.

2. According to the *New Earnings Survey* of 1976, 10.5 per cent of

those employed in East Anglia were in the Agriculture, Forestry and Fishing sector, compared to the national average of 2.6 per cent. Further, average gross weekly earnings for those in this sector were £6.00 lower in East Anglia than the sector's national average.

3. *Small Towns Study,* Cambridgeshire and Ely County Council, 1972, 83. Manufacturing industry provided only 23 per cent of total employment—about 1,600 jobs—approximately a third of which were for women. *Ibid.,* Table 15, p. 85.

4. Between 1961–1971, the number of holdings with over 500 acres increased from 44 to 72 (*ibid.,* p. 83).

5. This figure was suggested on 1975 data by Field (ed.), 1976:12–14.

6. Since 1966 unemployment rates for Fakenham have averaged 1–2 per cent higher than East Anglian rates as a whole, with extreme seasonal fluctuations (Fig. 14, *ibid.*)

7. To my knowledge, there is no study charting the evolution of the sexual division of labour in the shoe industry. One can only presume that it would bear a resemblance to clothing, where changes in the labour process have resulted in the concentration of women onto assembly processes and the sewing machine, and the concentration of men in the cutting room. In an excellent article on sex and skill in the organisation of the clothing industry, Coyle (1982) explains why it is women who are still confined to unskilled and low-paid work within the industry, whilst men hold on to a diminishing range of jobs which are accepted as skilled work and men's work.

8. He added that '45 redundancies was a considerable number for a town the size of Fakenham'.

9. *Eastern Daily Press,* 21 March 1972.

10. Letter from NUFLAT Head Office, 20 April 1972.

11. *Eastern Daily Press,* 4 April 1972.

12. In 1971, for example, the figures for industrial stoppages show 26 workers involved per 1,000 employed in East Anglia, compared to 54 per 1,000 in Great Britain. That is, East Anglia is one of the regions least affected by stoppages.
Source: *Earnings, Other Incomes and Household Expenditure in East Anglia,* East Anglia Economic Planning Council, 1977.

13. Report for ICOM from Colin Johnson, 30 April 1972.

Chapter 4   *Profitability—The Immediate Priority?*

1. Pell Footwear was eventually closed down in August 1975, by its parent company, the Steinberg Group.
2. Section 8 of the 1972 Industry Act was the only one that might be applied. 'That section stipulates that the support to the enterprise must be in the national interest, be of benefit to the economy and that finance from other sources is not available.'
3. Indeed, it appears that it was Parkyn (a Scott Bader director) who suggested to Shingler and Thetford that they might consider acquiring the firm.
4. Scott Bader describes its control structure in the following terms:

> The shares are held by the Commonwealth in one inclusive certificate. Control is exercised by employees as members of the Commonwealth rather than as share-holders and capital in the firm is considered to be 'neutralised' not distributed among the members. The company is too large to practise direct democracy and control operates through a representative structure. The firm is split into 15 constituencies. Each constituency elects one of its number to a body called the Community Council. The Council has final authority in the event of a dispute, approves directors and elects two of its members to the Board of Directors. The Board of Directors has authority from the general meeting to run the company. Its members are nominated by the chairman and approved by the community council. The Board appoints managers to carry out its policy *as in any conventional company* [my emphasis].

The Board of Directors, accountable to the Commonwealth, is responsible for the overall administration and control. This is achieved, however, by quarterly meetings of all the employees and, therefore, the board has considerable power. In practice, the community council has the power to veto and also may make recommendations to the board. Godric Bader, who has succeeded his father as Chairman of Scott Bader, has the power to appoint eight out of the ten directors (subject to the approval of the community council). In 1951, four members of the Bader family were directors. The Bader family are still the main force in Scott Bader.
5. Transcript of tapes made by D. Glass, Warwick University Modern Records Centre, their ref. 37/8–9.

6. Rowen Ltd was set up in 1965 and employs about 15. It is a co-operative, a member of ICOM, and got financial assistance from Scott Bader in 1970. The firm manufactures outdoor furniture.

7. Wage systems in the footwear industry have been essentially piece-work or incentive dominated, and this is particularly the case in the closing rooms. For details, see Goodman *et al.* (1977).

8. Letter from Brian Parkyn to Michael Ward—25 May 1973.

> I must say in confidence that I was not unimpressed with Richard Hicks. He is clearly the only person with the time and ability to help put Fakenham Enterprises Ltd onto a sound financial basis and provided we, as the Board, can strike the right balance between giving him complete freedom of executive action on the one hand and over much control on the other, I think there is a possibility (and I would still only rate it as a possibility) that it might be possible for the company to be commercially viable in a short time.

9. Report on Fakenham Enterprises—10 March 1973. Written by Hicks.

> This company should expect no different consideration from any other because of its co-ownership status. The writer has understood co-ownership to mean exactly that—co-ownership—that the shares of the Company are owned by its employees in equal parts. That the ownership of these shares entitles each member, as a shareholder, to vote at the Annual General Meeting for the appointment or removal of the Directors and Officers of the Company, and the other items on the Agenda, and have the rights of any normal shareholder. That the Directors of the Company, being the Board, formulate the policy to be carried out, for, and on behalf of the shareholders. That the shareholder's special advantage is, that being employees they are therefore more informed and nearer the Company than is usual, and can contribute by helping and advising the Directors in formulating policies.

10. According to many of the women's comments, as well as Michael Ward's below:
"The girls couldn't stand him . . ."

11. In a letter to Godric Bader from Nancy—date unknown:

> I must set out a few facts about Hicks' appointment as our general manager. It is a fact that we were informed in the nicest possible

way that if we had no manager we would have no further injections
of capital from Scott Bader . . . we thought Scott Bader would
liquidate us. Hicks has been anything but a good manager.

12. Nancy complained to the board about Hicks' infrequent visits
to Fakenham at irregular intervals: 'one cannot manage a factory
by remote control'.

Chapter 5   *The Fakenham Women*

1. All wage figures refer to weekly take-home pay for 1975,
unless specified otherwise. At this time, the national average
gross weekly earnings for full-time male manual workers was
£54.
Source: *New Earnings Survey,* 1975.
2. The Union had no strike funds, so men with working wives
did not get any money.
3. Edna is here referring to the local food-processing factories,
which were the main source of employment for women in
Fakenham.

Chapter 6   *Going it Alone*

1. For details of the very low rates paid to homeworkers in the
clothing industry, see Brown (1974).
2. For a vivid account of the tyranny of piecework, which is the
common experience of most women factory workers, see Herzog
(1980).
3. Olive: 'You're not under pressure to work like when you are
working for piece-work rate—where it's all heads down and one
against the other.'
4. Time studies are common practice in the clothing industry.
For example, see *Work Study in the Clothing Industry* (NEDO
publication).
5. For a detailed account of the period, see Lockett (1978).

Chapter 7 *Wives, Mothers, Workers*

1. For details, see Chapter 3. Nancy is an exception, and she will be discussed later.
2. These five life–cycle stages are outlined in the life–cycle section of Chapter 1.
3. See Table 1 in Chapter 5. Molly and Isabel are exceptions.
4. This latter interpretation is given added plausibility by Gillespie (1972) and Pahl (1980).
5. See Barrett and McIntosh (1980), Campbell and Charlton (1978), and Land (1980). For a critique of the concept of the household in neoclassical economics, see Galbraith (1974: Chapter IV).
6. Here Young provides some information about the uneven distribution of income between husbands and wives in working–class families, which operates to the economic disadvantage of wives and children. Pahl (1980) has more recently reviewed further evidence for Young's thesis. For a discussion of the limitations of official surveys, such as the *Family Expenditure Survey,* which take the household as the unit of analysis and, thus, fail to provide information about the distribution of income and wealth within the family, see the Equal Opportunities Commission's report based on evidence to 'The Royal Commission on Income Distribution and Wealth' (1977) and Land (1981).
7. By doing more housework, such as mending clothes and buying less prepared foods, housewives can reduce household expenses to some extent. See Gardiner *et al.* (1976).
8. Pahl (1980) and Hunt (1978, 1980) provide evidence for the existence of a wide variety of family budgeting systems. But they both conclude that, whichever system is used, the husband has the final say over how money is spent.
9. A critical consideration of this study, which argues that the husband still controls most of the power decisions in the family, is provided by Gillespie (1972).
10. Again, see Pahl (1980) and Hunt (1978, 1980). This point was consistently confirmed by the Fakenham women.
11. See Land (1981), as noted in footnote 3, Chapter 1.
12. It may be of interest here to note a survey on the effects of inflation on housekeeping allowances in Bethnal Green, even though the working–class women involved were not working.

The authors found that there was a 'tendency for wives to suffer, relatively to their husbands, in any period of inflation', as nearly half their sample of wives had not received any extra money from their husbands even though most of the husbands were earning higher wages (Syson and Young, 1974:110).

13. This is analagous to the rural tradition of women taking their children with them to do agricultural work. See, for example, Samuel (1975) for a description of women farm workers in East Anglia and Norfolk in the second half of the nineteenth century.

14. Although this point is generally assumed and not tested. One exception to this is Cunnison's work. She had both men and women in her sample and she did ask them this question. She reports, 'Even so, for the married women, unless they were breadwinners, there was not the same sense of the inevitability of working that there was for the men. Three married women told me that they came out to work "for the company". No man ever said this.' (Cunnison, 1966:85).

15. For a suggestive, if preliminary, attempt to theorise the means by which husbands maintain their traditional authority over wives, and the strategies they employ in attempting to ensure the stability of their power, see Bell and Newby (1976). As an instance of such a strategy, they quote Mauss on gift relationships as follows:

> To give is to show one's superiority, to show that one is something more and higher, that one is magister. To accept without returning or repaying more is to face subordination, to become a client and subservient, to become minister
>
> (Bell and Newby, 1976:162).

Chapter 8   *Experience and Consciousness*

1. Newby (1979) was looking at the issue of 'deference', which was about individuals who subscribe to a moral order which legitimises their own political, material and social subordination. Newby's criticism of the concept of deference and the interpretation that he gives to his data tends, however, to be limited by implicit assumptions of dual consciousness.

2. Newby (1979) provides a useful review of debates about the constitution of working-class consciousness in Britain, with special reference to the concept of 'deference'. As he puts it, there

was a tendency 'to slide from deference, as indicated by working-class Toryism, to false consciousness and back again' (Newby, 1979:108).

3. See, for example, Mann (1970, 1973); Blackburn and Mann (1975); Nichols and Armstrong (1976); Lane and Roberts (1971); Hyman (1973); and Newby (1979).

4. See Hunt (1980); Pollert (1981); Porter (1982).

5. See Stewart and Blackburn (1975); Prandy (1979); Holmwood and Stewart (1979); and Stewart *et al.* (1980).

Bibliography

Abercrombie, N. and Turner, B., 'The dominant ideology thesis', *British Journal of Sociology,* Vol. XXIX, No. 2, June 1978.

Barratt Brown, M., Coates, K. and Topham, T., 'Workers' control versus "revolutionary" theory', in R. Miliband and J. Saville (eds.), *The Socialist Register 1975,* Merlin Press.

Barrett, M. and McIntosh, M., 'The "family wage": Some problems for socialists and feminists', *Capital and Class,* No. 11, 1980.

Barrett, M., *Women's Oppression Today,* Verso, 1980.

Bechhofer, F. and Elliott, B., 'Petty property: the survival of a moral economy', in Bechhofer and Elliott (ed.), *The Petite Bourgeoisie,* St. Martin's Press, 1981.

Bell, B., 'Fighting for Survival', *The Observer,* 17/4/1977.

Bell, C. and Newby, H., 'Husbands and wives: the dynamics of the deferential dialectic', in D. Barker and S. Allen (eds.), *Dependence and Exploitation in Work and Marriage,* Longman, 1976.

Beynon, H and Blackburn, R.M., *Perceptions of Work,* Cambridge University Press, 1972.

Blackburn, R.M. and Mann, M., 'Ideology in the non-skilled working class', in M. Bulmer (ed.), *Working-Class Images of Society,* Routledge and Kegan Paul, 1975.

Blackburn, R.M. and Mann, M., *The Working Class in the Labour Market,* Macmillan, 1979.

Blood, R. and Wolfe, D., *Husbands and Wives,* Free Press, 1960.

Blum, F., *Work and Community: SBC and the Quest for a New Social Order,* Routledge and Kegan Paul, 1968.

Blumberg, P., *Industrial Democracy: The Sociology of Participation,* Constable, 1968.

Braverman, H., *Labour and Monopoly Capital,* Monthly Review Press, 1974.

Brown, R., 'Women as employees: some comments on research in industrial sociology', in D. Barker and S. Allen (eds.), *Dependence and Exploitation in Work and Marriage,* Longman, 1976.

Campbell, B. and Charlton, V., 'Work to rule—wages and the family', *Red Rag,* 1978.

Cavendish, R., *Women on the Line,* Routledge and Kegan Paul, 1982.

Chaplin, P. and Cowe, R., *A survey of contemporary British worker co-operatives,* Working Papers No. 36, Manchester Business School, 1977.

Clarke, T., 'Industrial democracy: The institutionalised suppression of industrial conflict?', in T. Clarke and L. Clements (eds.), *Trade Unions Under Capitalism,* Fontana, 1977.

Clegg, H.A., *A New Approach to Industrial Democracy,* Blackwell, 1960.

Coates, K. (ed.), *Can the Workers Run Industry?* Sphere Books, 1968.

Coates, K., 'Democracy and Workers' Control', *Towards Socialism,* Fontana, 1965.

Coates, K. (ed.), *Can the Workers Run Industry?,* Sphere Books, 1968.

Coates, K. and Topham, T., *The New Unionism,* Penguin, 1974.

Coates, K. (ed.), *The New Worker Co-operatives,* Spokesman Books, 1976.

Cockburn, C., *Brothers: Male Dominance and Technological Change,* Pluto, 1983.

Coyle, A., 'Sex and skill in the organisation of the clothing industry', in J. West (ed.), *Work, Women and the Labour Market,* Routledge & Kegan Paul, 1982.

Cressey, P. and MacInnes, J., '"Voting for Ford": Industrial democracy and the control of labour', *Capital and Class,* No. 11, 1980.

Cunnison, S., *Wages and Work Allocation,* Tavistock, 1966.

Dubin, R., 'Industrial workers' worlds: A study of the 'central life interests' of industrial workers', *Social Problems,* 3, 1956.

Eccles, T., *Under New Management,* Pan, 1981.

Edelstein, J.D., 'The origin, structure, and problems of four British producers' co-operatives', unpublished paper, presented at the A.S.A. Conference, New York, 1976.

Feldberg, R. and Glenn, E., 'Male and female: job versus gender models in the sociology of work', *Social Problems,* No. 26, 1979.

Field, F. (ed.), *Are Low Wages Inevitable?* Spokesman Books, 1976.

Flanders, A., Pomeranz, R. and Woodward, J., *Experiment in Industrial Democracy*, Faber and Faber, 1968.

Fogarty, M., Rapoport, R. and Rapoport, R., *Sex, Career and Family*, Allen and Unwin, 1971.

Fox, A., *A History of the National Union of Boot and Shoe Operatives: 1874–1957*, Blackwell, 1958.

Galbraith, J.K., *Economics and the Public Purpose*, Deutsch, 1974.

Gardiner, J., Himmelweit, S. and Mackintosh, M., 'Women's domestic labour', *On the Political Economy of Women*, CSE Pamphlet, No. 2, 1976.

Gillespie, D., 'Who has the power? The marital struggle', in H. Dreitzel (ed.), *Family, Marriage, and the Struggle of the Sexes*, Macmillan, 1972.

Goodman, J.F.B., Armstrong, E.G.A., Davis, J.E. and Wagner, A., *Rule-Making and Industrial Peace*, Croom Helm, 1977.

Hadden, T., *Company Law and Capitalism*, Weidenfield and Nicolson, 1972.

Herzog, M., *From Hand to Mouth*, Penguin, 1980.

HMSO, *Social Trends*, 1982.

Holmwood, J. and Stewart, A., *Central Issues in British Stratification*, Department of Applied Economics, Mimeo, Cambridge, 1979.

Huckfield, L., 'Riding it out at Meriden', *Personnel Management*, September, 1974.

Hunnius, G., Garson, G. David and Case, J., *Workers' Control*, Vintage Books, 1973.

Hunt, P., 'Cash-transactions and household tasks', *Sociological Review*, Vol. 26, 3, 1978.

Hunt, P., *Gender and Class Consciousness*, Macmillan, 1980.

Hyman, R., 'Industrial conflict and the political economy', in R. Miliband and J. Saville (eds.), *The Socialist Register, 1973*, Merlin Press.

Hyman, R., 'Workers' Control and Revolutionary Theory', in R. Miliband and J. Saville, *The Socialist Register, 1974*, Merlin Press.

Jephcott, P., Seear, N. and Smith, J.H., *Married Women Working*, Allen and Unwin, 1962.

Jessop, R.D., *Traditionalism, Conservatism and British Political Culture*, Allen and Unwin, 1974.

Jones, D., 'British producer co-operatives', in K. Coates (ed.), *The New Worker Co-operatives*, Spokesman Books, 1976.

Kaluzynska, E., 'Wiping the floor with theory—a survey of writings on housework', *Feminist Review*, No. 6, 1980.

Klein, V., *Britain's Married Women Workers*, Routledge and Kegan Paul, 1965.

Land, H., *Parity Begins at Home*, EOC/SSRC Joint Panel, 1981.

Land, H., 'The Family Wage', *Feminist Review*, No. 6, 1980.

Lane, T. and Roberts, K., *Strike at Pilkingtons*, Fontana, 1971.

Lockett, M., *Fakenham Enterprises*, Co-operatives Research Monograph I, The Open University, 1978.

Logan, C. and Gregory, D., *Co-operatives and Job Creation in Wales*, Wales TUC, 1981.

Lupton, T., *On the Shop Floor*, Pergamon Press, 1963.

Mandel, E., 'Self-management—dangers and possibilities', *International*, Vol. 2, No. 3, Winter/Spring 1975.

Mann, M., *Consciousness and Action among the Western Working Class*, Macmillan, 1973.

Mann, M., 'The social cohesion of liberal democracy', *American Sociological Review*, Vol. 35, No. 3, June 1970.

Moore, E., *Bullock and Britain*, unpublished M.A. dissertation, Essex University, 1977.

Myrdal, A. and Klein, V., *Women's Two Roles*, Routledge and Kegan Paul, 1956.

Newby, H., *The Deferential Worker*, Penguin, 1979.

Nichols, T. and Armstrong, P., *Workers Divided*, Fontana, 1976.

Oakeshott, R., *The Case for Workers' Co-ops*, Routledge and Kegan Paul, 1978.

Oakley, A., *Housewife*, Penguin Books, 1976.

Oakley, A., *Subject Women*, Martin Robertson, 1981.

Oakley, A., *The Sociology of Housework*, Martin Robertson, 1974.

Pahl, J., 'Patterns of money management within marriage', *Journal of Social Policy*, Vol. 9, July 1980.

Parkin, F., *Class Inequality and Political Order*, Paladin, 1972.

Pelly, D., 'Worker co-operatives—new wave on an old beach', unpublished paper, presented at the Alternative Strategies for the Labour Movement Conference, October 1981.

Phillips, A. and Taylor, B., 'Sex and skill: Notes towards a feminist economics', *Feminist Review*, No. 6, 1980.

Pollert, A., *Girls, Wives, Factory Lives*, Macmillan, 1981.

Porter, M., Standing on the edge: Working class housewives and the world of work', in J. West (ed.), *Work, Women and the Labour Market*, Routledge and Kegan Paul, 1982.

Prandy, K., 'Alienation and interests in the analysis of social cognitions', *British Journal of Sociology,* Vol. XXX, No. 4, December 1979.

Purcell, K., 'Militancy and acquiescence amongst women workers', in S. Burman (ed.), *Fit Work for Women,* Croom Helm, 1979.

Rapoport, R. and Rapoport, R., *Dual-Career Families,* Penguin Books, 1971.

Rose, D., Saunders, P., Newby, H. and Bell, C., 'Ideologies of property: A case study', *Sociological Review,* Vol. 24, No. 4, November, 1976.

Samuel, R. (ed.), *Village Life and Labour,* Routledge and Kegan Paul, 1975.

Scargill, A., *A Debate on Workers' Control,* Institute of Workers' Control Pamphlets, April, 1978.

Scase, R. and Goffee, R., *The Entrepreneurial Middle Class,* Croom Helm, 1982.

Siltanen, J., 'A commentary on theories of female wage labour', Cambridge Women's Studies Group, *Women in Society,* Virago, 1981.

Stewart, A. and Blackburn, R.M., 'The stability of structural inequality', *The Sociological Review,* Vol. 23, No. 3, 1975.

Stewart, A., Prandy, K. and Blackburn, R.M., *Social Stratification and Occupations,* Macmillan, 1980.

Syson, L. and Young, M., 'Poverty in Bethnal Green', in M. Young (ed.), *Poverty Report 1974,* Temple Smith.

Taylor, R., 'Meriden co-op is given a deadline', *The Observer,* 29 July, 1979.

Thornley, J., *Workers' Co-operatives,* Heinemann, 1981.

Tomlinson, J., 'British politics and co-operatives', *Capital and Class,* No. 12, 1980/81.

Wajcman, J., 'Work and the family: Who gets the best of both worlds?', Cambridge Women's Studies Group, *Women in Society,* Virago, 1981.

Wajcman, J., 'Review article', *Capital and Class,* No. 18, 1982/1983.

Wainwright, H., 'Women and the division of labour', in P. Abrams (ed.), *Work, Urbanism and Inequality,* Weidenfeld and Nicolson, 1978.

Westergaard, J. and Resler, H., *Class in a Capitalist Society,* Heinemann, 1975.

Willis, P., *Learning to Labour,* Saxon House, 1977.

Vanek, J., *The General Theory of Labour-Managed Market Economies,* Cornell University Press, 1970.

Vanek, J. (ed.), *Self-Management,* Penguin, 1975.

Young, M., 'Distribution of income within the family', *British Journal of Sociology,* 3, 1952.

Young, M. and Willmott, P., *The Symmetrical Family,* Penguin Books, 1975.

Yudkin, S. and Holme, A., *Working Mothers and Their Children,* Michael Joseph, 1963.